Doug Sa

ACTION ON THE FIRST TEE

Doug Sanders'

ACTION ON THE FIRST TEE

How to Cash In On Your Favorite Sport

with Russ Pate

Taylor Publishing
Dallas, Texas

This book is dedicated to anyone who's ever had to pay off in the 19th hole.

Special thanks to Hyatt Bear Creek East for its kind assistance and support.

Copyright 1987 © by S & B Partners, Inc.

Library of Congress Cataloging-in-Publication Data

Sanders, Doug, 1933-
☐ The action on the first tee.

☐ Includes index.
☐ 1. Golf — Betting.   I. Pate, Russ.   II. Title.
GV965.S238   1987   796.352   87-1927
ISBN 0-87833-551-X

Printed in the United States of America
9 8 7 6 5 4 3 2

Design: Blackbirch Graphics, Inc.

CONTENTS

Acknowledgments

I'd like to thank the following people for their contributions to this book:

My fellow touring pros and good friends Al Balding, George Bayer, John Brodie, Jim Cochran, Bruce Crampton, Lee Elder, Jack Fleck, Raymond Floyd, Doug Ford, Bob Goalby, Peter Jacobson, Ted Kroll, Charlie Owens, Arnold Palmer, Gary Player, Bob Rosburg, Chi-Chi Rodriguez, Ben Smith, Sam Snead, Mike Souchak, Lee Trevino, Ken Venturi and Walt Zembriski.

Club professionals Danny Silianoff of Crown Colony C.C. in Lufkin, Texas, Randy Smith of Royal Oaks C.C. in Dallas, Texas, and Larry Box of Bear Creek Resort in Irving, Texas.

Tour caddies "Crosshanded Jake" and "Puzzle," and veteran St. Andrews caddy John Sorley.

I also want to thank such notable personalities as Claude Akins, Ed Bruce, Mac Davis, Phil Harris, Mickey Newberry, Charles Price, Darrell Royal and Alan Shepard.

Amateur golfers and golf aficionados Bob Allen, Jim Baccus, Corley Barnes, Carlton Boren, Ben Burkett, Jerry W. Biesel, Elliott Bradley, Joe Clements, Stan Corbitt, Debbie Cartwright, Willard Dewveall, Bill Dixon, Richard Emery, Eric Gleacher, Howard Garrett, Leon Grivel, Jr., W.C. Hagan, III, Dr. James H. Hill, Bruce Jolesch, Joe T. Kelly, Bill King, Barney Larnier, Dr. Larry Leonard, Tommy Luckie, O.W. McCurdy, Charles "Bubba" Majors, Dick Martin, Terry Murphy, Bill Munn, Don Morrell, Doyle Morrow, Jeffrey Ohl, John Oram, Franklin Adams Pritchard, Chuck Reibling, Bill Roberts, J.D. Sandefer III, Lowell Slocum, Ray Stoker, Bill Saunders, Don Smith, Mack Strother, Dick Tartre, Rob Taylor, Rex Vardeman, Howard F. Van Zandt, Joel T. Williams, Mike Windham, Doyle Winters, Joel Wittenbraker, "Red" Whitehead, J.T. Yates and Bob Yeager.

I wish to thank Fred Oman, owner of The Investors' Gallery in Dallas, for helping research some of the material contained in the text and for providing the line art caricatures displayed throughout.

The references to Titanic Thompson are used with the permission of Richard C. Campbell and Sunbelt Productions, Inc., which holds the rights to Ti's life story and which plans to produce a biographical feature film. I don't get to see too many movies, but I'll make it a point to see that one.

Most of all, I'd like to thank Gary Boren, my friend and business partner. Gary serves as Chairman of the Doug Sanders International Junior Golf Championship, the largest junior event in the world. He originated the idea for this book and then was the driving force behind its publication.

Along with my co-author, Russ Pate, and my publisher, Taylor, I wish to thank them one and all.

Doug Sanders

Introduction

It's no secret that I'm a person who agrees with the old saying that variety is the spice of life. Variety is one of the things I've enjoyed most in my career as a professional golfer. It's helped make my career a pretty spicy one, I might add.

I've enjoyed the variety of people I've been introduced to through golf. From U.S. presidents and foreign heads of state to the top names in show business and sports. From the captains of industry to the guys who've made a living the same way I started out in golf—the caddies.

I've enjoyed the variety of personalities I've played with on the professional golf circuit. The characters like Jimmy Demaret and Tommy Bolt; the competitors like Arnold Palmer and Jack Nicklaus; the foreign stars like Gary Player and Roberto de Vicenzo; the storytellers like Sam Snead and Dutch Harrison; the showmen like Lee Trevino and Chi-Chi Rodriguez; the playboys like Al Besselink and Ray Floyd. (In the case of Raymond, I should stress that somewhere along the way golf lost a playboy and gained a great champion—and an even greater family man.)

I've enjoyed the variety of continents and countries I've visited to play in tournaments and in conjunction with my Doug Sanders International Junior Golf program, which conducts clinics and tournaments for kids while promoting junior golf worldwide. Kids that compete in my junior tournament, even if they don't become golf professionals, have a chance to win college scholarships so they can better themselves no matter what profession they choose to pursue. My junior program enables me to give back something to the sport that has been so good to me and my family. It's something of which I'm very proud, and it continues to get bigger each year.

I've also enjoyed variety in my golf apparel. Although I wear bright colors primarily to please myself, I've found that my clothes always helped me establish an immediate rapport with galleries. People have enjoyed checking out my coordinated outfits for as long as I've been wearing them.

I've always tried to dress as colorfully as I can, but there is no special pattern to what I put on. If I have a blasé feeling some morning, I might choose bright colors to give me an extra spark that day. If I feel strong and aggressive when I arise, I'll probably put on an ensemble highlighted by a dominant color to match my mood. Unlike players like Gary Player, who preferred all-black, or Lee Trevino, who liked to play the final round wearing red and black, I've never been superstitious about any one color. I've won tournaments wearing all color combinations, and at one time or another I've three-putted in all of them, too.

For the past 30 years, wherever professional golf has taken me, galleries have stopped, looked, and listened. Stopped and looked at my clothes, listened to me joke around. I've made thousands of friends through the years, strangers who came out of curiosity to see who and what Doug Sanders was all about.

Anyway, it was my fondness for variety and fresh approaches in life that made me immediately receptive when Gary Boren approached me with the idea for this book. Gary, who's an avid amateur player, sought my help in compiling a comprehensive list of different games golfers play and the wagers they make. He told me he was feeling burned out with the sameness of his standard Saturday game and wanted to develop a variety of alternatives for his golf outings. He was certain more options would mean more enjoyment.

Gary correctly assumed that Doug Sanders was the kind of guy who would have played many of them or at least would have heard about most of the others. I've been hanging out at golf courses almost every day since the early 1940s; I guarantee that you hear a lot of stories and meet a lot of characters that way.

Sure, I said to Gary, let's give it a go. We mapped out a plan to do this book on golf games and gamesmanship, as well as a second book on golf characters and stories from that bygone era of golf hustling. Golf stories are a lot like fish stories—there's a million of them, and a few of the big ones always get away—but I've already started putting together a string of keepers. I'm eager to preserve for the record an important chapter in the history of golf. While you're working your way through the golf games in this book, be keeping an eye out for that second book as well.

Our search for golf games uncovered more than *100* ways to gamble, as well as dozens more than we tossed out for not being up to par. On the following pages you'll be able to read a description of each game and its rules for play.

As you might suspect, golfers around the country play many of the same games. Nassau, Skins, and Round-Robins with Low Ball or Low Ball/Low Total are popular in virtually all regions. But we've found some exotics—games like Oklahoma Whip-Out, Reno Putts, Hammer, Snake, and Wolf—that many golfers may not have tried.

The point to remember is that having a variety of golf games from which to select will increase your enjoyment of the sport. I'd suggest you spend several rounds working your way through different games to find the ones you and your playing partners like best.

One of my personal goals for *Doug Sanders' Action on the First Tee* is to give every golfer at least one game—and preferably more—that he can take to the bank. Every reader should discover a game that's suited to his ability and temperament. These golf games run the gamut from driving games to putting games to chipping games to 19th hole games, and somewhere down the line a reader will hit on something at which he'll be a winner.

Another goal is to give readers a slant on how to gain the winner's edge. Beginning on page 147, I'll share some of my insights and experience on how to play winning golf within your regular group.

I'll talk about the most critical quality a golfer must possess: *Patience*. About knowing when to press the advantage and when to back away from a foolish proposition. To know when to hold 'em and when to fold 'em, in other words.

It's one thing to be outplayed at golf and another thing to be outsmarted. We all have days when we don't play to the best of our abilities and can be beaten physically. But there's never a valid excuse for having a letdown mentally. Keep your wits about you, know yourself and your own game, and I guarantee you can get a long-term lease sitting in the catbird seat.

The main goal of this book, though, is to help golfers derive more satisfaction and enjoyment from the game. If I can succeed in doing that, I'll consider this undertaking to have been a success.

Warming Up

There's a famous story about Walter Hagen, as much of a legend off the golf course as he was on it, that in one PGA tournament he arrived at the first tee dressed in a tuxedo.

Hagen had been out partying all night, as he liked to do from time to time, and he had to go directly to the golf course so as not to miss his tee time. Hagen arrived at the first tee with seconds to spare. Without removing his satin-trimmed jacket, he hit a towering drive straight down the middle of the fairway. Then he casually slipped out of his formal wear, slipped into his golfing attire and shot a smooth 67 that day.

Hagen was the original "stop and smell the roses" guy. Of course he also liked the smell of bonded whiskey and the fragrance of a woman's perfume. The Haig, as he was called, set a standard for partying, which several of us who followed him down the PGA's golden road have aspired to. I know that by trying to emulate Hagen I was ready for the PGA's Senior Tour by the time I was 35.

On the morning of his 1926 PGA championship match with Leo
Diegel at the Salisbury G.C. on Long Island, Hagen came strolling
into his mid-Manhattan hotel at roughly 4 a.m. He'd been out sampling
the good life that New York City had to offer. It *was* the Roaring
Twenties, after all.

A sportswriter from one of the dailies, camped out at the lobby bar
like all good press guys should be, stopped him.

"Hagen, where've you been all night? You've got a match to play
in a few hours."

"Yes, I know," sniffed Hagen. "I'll be ready."

"But Mr. Diegel's been in bed asleep for hours," said the scribe.

"He may have been in bed," Hagen replied dryly, "but I can assure you he hasn't been sleeping."

The mere thought of playing the great Walter Hagen could be a fitful experience, indeed. The Haig proceeded to toss and turn Diegel 5 and 3 in the 36-hole match-play final for his third consecutive PGA title.

As much as I admired The Haig for his style and panache, I certainly can't condone the incident where he headed for the first tee without properly warming up. I hope you're not the kind of player that rushes to the course, hurriedly changes clothes or throws on his golf shoes, and races for the first tee.

You need to slow down.

If you show up in a rush, you'll probably play in a rush. Your tempo will likely be too fast all day, and that will produce some problems with your swing. You're liable to be easy pickings for your playing partners.

Instead of heading for your golf game in a mad dash, I would advise you to plan to arrive at the course at least an hour ahead of your tee time. That way you can set about your business in a purposeful, but unhurried, manner.

Unless the course where you play has no practice facility, you should make it a rule to hit a bucket of balls before you play. Personally, I like to spend 30 minutes warming up by hitting balls and then another 15 minutes putting on the practice green.

Basically, in those 45 minutes I'm trying to achieve a feeling of looseness and flexibility, while relieving any tension that might have accumulated from the previous night.

Like a hangover, for example.

There's the old story about the time my pals Phil Harris and Dean Martin staggered out to the first tee at the Las Vegas Country Club after pulling an all-nighter. Harris, who could barely get his ball teed up, took a couple of practice swings and then addressed the ball.

He swung, and missed completely. He promptly resumed his stance and swung again. Another miss.

"That's it," said Harris. "I'm not playing today."

"Don't quit now, Phil," advised Martin. "You've got a no-hitter going."

Like a lot of golf stories, that one might not have happened. If indeed it did, Phil could have used a warm-up session with a pot of black coffee.

I wish to emphasize that there's a vast difference between warming up for a round and practicing. Though many golfers fail to make that distinction, it's a critical one.

Warming up is a method for getting the muscles attuned for the task at hand. You want to check the overall swing for timing and feel without checking the individual parts. All you want to accomplish by warming up is to create a feeling of being loose, relaxed and eager to play a round of golf.

Practicing is an entirely different matter. It's an intensive work session where you break down the elements of your swing with the intention of correcting specific flaws.

I've found that the best time for practicing is immediately after a round of golf, provided that you haven't celebrated too long—or drowned too many sorrows—in the 19th hole. While settling your bets and engaging in some friendly banter about the day's game, you should mentally conduct a shot-by-shot analysis of your round.

You want to isolate the areas where you wasted strokes, because practicing should be devoted to addressing those problem areas. Maybe you weren't making a good shoulder turn. Maybe you were hanging back on your right side and not making a good weight transfer into the shot. Maybe you hit the ball crisply all day but were misaligned on most of your shots.

There's a thousand things that can go wrong with the golf swing—but fortunately there also happen to be a thousand cures. The practice tee is the best place to get the problems worked out.

By the way, there's no good reason to hang around the practice area hitting sweet shot after sweet shot. The only person you'll impress is yourself. I much prefer to save the best shots for the course—where they can win me some money.

Once the flaws have been corrected and your swing has been re-grooved, work on some other facet like chipping or pitching. If your practice facility has a sand trap or two, practice your bunker shots.

The point I want to stress is that at the end of any practice session, you should feel a sense of accomplishment. You should leave the practice tee with a positive feeling that you've added an element to your game that can be called upon the next time you tee it up.

Don't ever leave the golf course after a tough day feeling like the game has got you whipped. Believe me, golf's tough enough when you're in a positive frame of mind. A negative attitude will make it impossible for you to play your best. Remember there's always going to be another day and another game, so even on the days you play your worst golf, you should try not to dwell on the negative.

My years of experience have convinced me that the best procedure a player can follow is to get to the golf course early, warm up properly, play each shot and each round to the best of your ability that day, and before heading home do some remedial work on the areas that beg for attention.

Then you can go ahead and enjoy your evening. Just like a Walter Hagen or a Doug Sanders would.

The Action on the First Tee

Warming up for a game of golf serves to accomplish more than lim-
bering up the muscles. It provides an opportunity to take a quick
inventory of your game.

Are you feeling especially sharp—or dull? Are the juices flowing?
How's your timing? Are you hitting the ball in the sweet spot or can
you feel that your swing mechanics are slightly off?

Golf is largely a game of mistakes. The winner—the guy my pal
Tommy Bolt likes to call "the guy who gets the cheese"—generally
isn't the guy who hits the most great shots. The winner, nine times
out of ten, is the guy who hits the fewest poor shots.

The winner will likely be the player who keeps his mistakes in play.
In bounds, out of hazards, and in a position from which he can recover.
The winner avoids the big mistakes.

As you're warming up, therefore, you should take stock of how well you're maneuvering the ball. Are you able to draw the ball when you want to? How about your fade, is it working too? Most golf courses require a variety of shots, both left-to-right and right-to-left. On windy days, are you able to hit both high shots (for downwind holes) and low ones (for going upwind)?

How well you strike the ball while warming up should help you plan your gambling strategy for that given day. A good, solid warmup session may suggest you'd be wise to raise your normal stakes. A sluggish warmup might be properly interpreted as a sign to keep the action low.

It's like being at the tables in Las Vegas. Sometimes you get on a hot streak and get a feeling that you can't lose a bet. That's when you want to increase your regular unit bet several times or more. At other times, when you feel lady luck disappearing, you want to limit your bet. Or better yet, cash in and take a hiatus.

On some days, after hitting no more than a half dozen shots, I'll know that it's going to be my day. I'll sense that I have my best rhythm and tempo and I know I can freewheel it straight at the flags. I'd take on anybody for any amount on those occasions.

At other times, though, my warm-up period will say to me, "Doug, there was no need to drag your tired ass out of bed, because, brother, this ain't your day." That's when you know immediately you'll have to grind it out for all 18 holes. I wouldn't want to give Rodney Dangerfield any strokes on those days.

Remember, golf isn't like the theaters on Broadway, where they say a lousy rehearsal means a great performance. In golf, a lousy rehearsal leads to a lousy performance. You can bet on it.

Warming up, incidentally, presents a prime window of opportunity to do some reconnaissance on your playing partners.

Watch to see how they are striking the ball that day. See if they look physically sharp—it's hard to hide a hangover or bloodshot eyes. Also be sure to read their body language and their demeanor for signs that they are mentally prepared, or unprepared, to play.

Who knows, your playing partners may be preoccupied with the details of impending business deals. Or maybe they've just had a spat with their wives or girl friends. Or maybe both. You never know.

Then again, if your playing partners don't warm up, if they come roaring out to the course in the hurry-up mode that you've now learned to avoid, you have a built-in advantage over them. Use it.

It's a rare player who can head straight to the first tee and make a complete adjustment from what he was doing a half-hour before. He'll likely need several holes to settle into his game. You should penalize him for his tardiness by changing the terms of the game.

The point I wish to highlight is that you should never arrive at the first tee in cavalier fashion, without a clue as to how you're going to play that day. The first tee is where you get down to business, and arriving unprepared is as inexcusable as if a corporate executive showed up at a board meeting without having looked at the agenda.

The first tee is where the action is in golf. It's traditionally the site at which bets are made. Standard games like Nassaus or Low-Ball are agreed on, side action like "Trash" or "Hold the Box" are added to the package of wagers, and before any balls are in the air everyone in the group must agree to the games and terms.

How you act on the first tee can create an immediate psychological advantage or disadvantage, especially if you're playing with a group of strangers. If you're aggressive, you can set them back on their heels. If you're too passive, however, you can give them an unwarranted air of confidence.

I learned that lesson years ago, when as a 13-year-old I showed up to play in the Georgia State Junior tournament for the first time. I swaggered up to the first tee and told my opponent, a local kid from Augusta, that I would play him a $5 Nassau. My bravura startled him so much that his hands started to shake. I had the match won even before the first ball was hit.

On infrequent occasions, you'll see or hear about groups that will play several holes before getting down to the business of golf gambling. That way, everyone has a clue of how he's playing and what games he's best suited for. As a rule, though, bets are firmed up on the first tee, and adjustments are seldom made before the turn.

Many of the most popular golf games involve partnerships or teams, and probably the most time-honored tradition to determine those alignments is to toss balls in the air.

The ball toss can have a variety of methods and interpretations.

23

The balls usually are collected by one player (the honor rotates), who then shakes them up in both hands and gives them an underhanded toss maybe 10 feet into the air.

The players in your group wait for the balls to drop and then "read" the results. Some players prefer to pair the owners of the two balls that are closest together. (Some like to pair the owners of the two balls closest together without touching.) Others prefer to pair the two balls that are farthest apart. All I can say is suit yourself.

The key point with the action on the first tee is that everyone in the game must be comfortable with the terms of the wager. As I mention elsewhere in this book there are times when players get in over their heads. Everyone has a comfort zone and a danger zone for his golf gambling, and it's each player's responsibility to stay within the one and well short of the other.

I have a pet saying that I think sums up this situation: "Don't let your alligator mouth overload your canary ass."

As far as I'm concerned there's only one thing worse than a player who gets snookered into bets he has no business making: a player who tries to pass off I.O.U.s to cover his debts.

If you're prepared to take another man's money, you need to be prepared to part with your own. That's why I like a golf game like Oklahoma Whip–Out (page 99) where all the bets are settled at the end of each hole.

Once up in Butte, Montana, I was playing a friendly game with my buddy Evel Kneivel, the daredevil. I call Evel "Devil," and he calls me "Angel." We were playing for three grand a hole, and the Devil let his ego get out of hand. I'd already won a couple of bets when he started some side action, betting $1,500 on the side that he could make par a particular hole. I accepted the bet. Poor Evel had to work hard to make his bogey.

Now he's getting mad. He wants to double the bet again on the next hole, so I said, "Why not?" Again, he fails to make par.

Now I know the Devil is down $13,000 and I know he's out of money because that's how much he showed me on the first tee.

"Three grand more on this next hole," says Evel, as we headed for the tee.

"Devil," I shot back, "I ain't no Angel of Mercy. I need to see some cash."

Evel owned a beautiful house overlooking the course we were playing, and before the game continued I made him send over to the house for more cash. I just stood around and told a few jokes to the gallery—we were playing in his celebrity event—while we waited for the infusion of capital.

I had no intention of winning any money that I couldn't collect on the spot. And Evel, being the perfect gentlemen that he is, understood my position fully.

But enough cracker-barrel philosophy from this old Georgia cracker. It's high time to *LET THE GAMES BEGIN.*

Standard Games

,

Nassau

The Nassau is unquestionably the most popular golf bet.

Played at either match-play or medal-play, the Nassau actually is three bets in one—the front nine, the back nine and the entire eighteen holes.

For example, a $2 Nassau would mean a player could win a maximum of $6 for the round. Two dollars for the front nine, two for the back nine and two for total score.

Many players, though, prefer to make the bet for the full eighteen holes double the amount of each nine-hole bet. In the example above, $4 would be riding on the round, and a player could win a maximum of $8.

Players who like more action than the Nassau will introduce a "Press," which in essence is a separate bet (see Presses). Some games are set up with automatic one-down presses, others with two-down presses.

The game of Nassau takes its name from the fact it was a popular game at one of America's first golfing clubs, Nassau Country Club on Long Island.

Low Ball

Low Ball is another of the standard bets of golf. As the name implies, the player who posts the low score on each hole wins that particular hole.

Low Ball can be used as a bet in a two-man match, with a unit bet— $2, $5, or whatever—applying to any hole that isn't halved (tied). Low Ball is a fun game for high-handicappers as well as low-handicappers. A double-bogey beats a triple just as decisively as a birdie beats a par or a par beats a bogey.

Low Ball is also a popular format for foursomes. It's often played with a round-robin format, where several partnerships are formed during a round.

I enjoy a game of Low Ball now and then, almost as much as I enjoy a game of Highball in the 19th hole.

Low Ball/Low Total

Low Ball/Low Total is a game frequently played by foursomes. It's a format that can be used for tournament play at private clubs or public links.

The game is scored according to points accumulated by a team. On each hole, a total of two points (one for Low Ball and one for Low Total) is at stake.

Typically, each point carries a value ($1, $2, $5, or whatever) players agree upon at the outset.

Let's look at some hypothetical examples using two two-player teams on a par-four hole:

If Team A shoots 4–4 for an 8 and Team B shoots 4–5 for a 9, only one point (for Low Total) is won. That's because Team B tied Team A for Low Ball.

If Team A shoots 3–6 for a 9 and Team B shoots 4–4 for an 8, the hole is a push. Team A wins Low Ball for its 3 and Team B wins Low total for its 8 so the bets effectively cancel each other out. (For scoring purposes, each team would receive one point.)

But if Team A shoots 3–4 for a 7 and Team B shots 4–4 for an 8, Team A takes away two bets. Low Ball (3) and Low Total (7).

At the end of the game, the points are added up, the difference calculated and the wagers settled. Low Ball/Low Total is a popular game because it keeps all the players involved in every hole. It's also a game that rewards consistency, since high scores on a hole usually mean the loss of one bet (Low Total) at the minimum.

Being careless or losing your concentration can become expensive in this game.

Robins

Robins, which is verbal shorthand for round-robins, are popular games to play within foursomes, especially for players who are playing with each other for the first time. Robins make a good get-acquainted game because at some point during the 18-hole round each player will be a partner with every other player in the group.

The Round-Robin system also distributes the talent within a foursome. If one member of the group is clearly superior to the others, his advantage will be shared by each of the others during the round.

The standard format is to play three 6-hole Robins within an 18-hole round, with all players paired once. Another option is to play six 3-hole robins, in which the players are paired twice with the other members of the foursome.

Robins are often played with either the low ball or low ball/low total determining who wins each hole. Other bets can be added to the package, of course.

The usual method for choosing the partners in a Robin is to toss balls at the first tee, with the owners of the two balls closest to each other forming the partnership. A ball toss is employed again at the 7th tee to form the partnerships for holes 7 thru 12. Partners for 13 thru 18 will be obvious.

Another frequent manner of selection, especially in areas where most players ride in golf carts, is to have cart mates team up on the first Robin, cart drivers team up on the second Robin and the drivers of one cart teamed with the rider of the other cart in the third Robin.

Players in the Northeast and Midwest have a novel way of playing Robins: they don't form the partnerships until the round is over.

While having cool beverage at the 19th hole, they pair up and then replay the round, calculating the bets for the partnerships.

Players also tell me that this method tends to improve everyone's competitiveness, since the feeling is similar to not having a partner, and as a result they tend to concentrate better during the round.

I'd venture to say that if you're eager to improve your overall game, this after-the-fact method is the best way to play Robins.

Presses

Mention the word *Press* to the average person and it might conjure the image of a guy who looks like Darren McGavin in a cheap suit and a fedora with a notebook in his hand and a camera around his neck, yelling "Wait! One More Comment!" on the steps of the county courthouse.

Some people might think of an ironing board or a Chinese laundry. Others might think of a full-court defense in basketball or Pete Maravich's father.

But to a golfer, the word *Press* means one thing only. *Press* signifies a new bet.

Pressing is a mechanism by which a losing player or team can try to get back in a match by starting a secondary wager.

The press is such an integral part of golf gambling that it is usually the first topic brought up after the game to be played is determined.

In most areas of the country, it is generally understood that unless one-down automatic presses or two-down automatics are specified, you cannot press unless you are two down.

If you do decide to press—nothing says you have to if they aren't "automatic"—make sure your opponent(s) acknowledge the new bet before play resumes. Also, don't wait until he is addressing the ball to press.

Some people do that to rattle their opponents, but to me it shows a lack of class. When a player has started setting up for a shot, be it a drive, an approach or a putt, all nearby movement and conversation should cease.

On the last hole, it's not uncommon for a player down several bets to suggest a "Press To Get Even." Unless that's agreed on at the outset, the player being pressed doesn't have to accept this bet—nor should he feel bad about turning it down.

As my pal Stan Dudas likes to say, "You've got to get out the way you got in."

Skins

Skins, one of the hottest new games in golf, is played where each hole has an assigned value, say $5, and the player who wins a hole outright with the low ball wins the pot.

If no player wins a hole outright—one tie, all tie as the saying goes—then the bet carries over to the next hole.

After several carryovers, the pot can reach a point where some players will show some dog and others will step up to meet the challenge. It's a good game for building character.

In some parts of the country, golfers call the game Cats. In other parts it's called Skats, a combination of the words Skins and Cats. It probably goes to show there's more than one way to skin a cat—or to separate your playing partners from some of their cash.

Regardless of what you call it, the game has become a favorite with amateurs ever since Don Ohlmeyer created "The Skins Game," a made-for-TV exhibition in which Arnold Palmer, Jack Nicklaus, and some of the PGA stars play for high stakes. Fuzzy Zoeller has been the big winner of the 1985 and 1986 Skins Games, pocketing something like $600,000. Hell, I wish they'd give other PGA Seniors a crack at that kind of cash.

By the way, out on the West Coast they play Skins where a hole won with a birdie earns double the original bet. In a game with carryovers and the birdie premium, you can have some serious money change hands.

Bingo Bango Bongo

This is one of the oldest and most popular games in golf. It's been around ever since I can remember, and probably a lot longer than that.

The game involves three points awarded on each hole. One point goes to the player whose ball is the first to come to rest on the clipped surface of the green (Bingo). One point goes to the player whose ball is nearest to the cup after all players reach the green (Bango). And one point goes to the player who's the first to hole out (Bongo).

Players in the Northeast, where the game originated, usually stipulate that if a player wins all three points, the bets are doubled, and if he wins all three points with a birdie on the hole, the bets are tripled.

My experience has been that Bingo Bango Bongo tends to even itself out during a round. The player who wins Bingo often loses Bango to a player who missed the green with his approach shot but then chips closer to the hole. Any player can win Bongo since there are no "gimmes" in this game.

Golfers of all abilities like Bingo Bango Bongo because there's plenty of action and seldom does anyone get burned. Besides, everyone in the group has something to shoot for on every hole.

Scotch
(Also known as Chicago or Five Points)

In the game of Scotch, each hole carries a possible total of five points.

Two points can be earned for the low ball and one point each for low total, greenies (see Trash), and natural birdies. If you win all five points for a hole, the bets are doubled and you in essence win 10 units.

Eric Gleacher, an investment banker in New York who played this game during his college days at Northwestern, helped explain its attraction to me. Although he couldn't recall where the name Scotch originated, he noted that the game is so popular in the Chicago area that many players call it "Chicago."

Sister games are called Six Point Scotch, where two points are awarded for natural birdies, and Seven Point Scotch, where two points are awarded for both natural birdies and greenies.

However Scotch is scored, its emphasis on natural birdies and greenies suggests it is best suited for top-flight players who prefer to play without adjusting for handicaps.

Getting Some on the Side

I've known some terrific golf gamblers who were lousy golfers themselves.

I mean *awful.* They'd take the club back in a convoluted arc, throw themselves at the ball with all the gracefulness of a drunk on a New York subway and take gouges out of God's green earth that would leave the fairways looking like gophers had moved in.

Those same guys drove up to the course in a shining new sedan, wore diamond rings on the little finger of their left hands and smoked Cuban cigars as thick as big bananas.

How did they do it?

Their secret for keeping their money clips full of cash was to have guys like me handle the playing while they handled the action.

By the time I reached my mid-teens, I was busting par by four or five shots every time out. That's when a couple of gamblers in Cedartown began setting up matches for me.

I'd play for $500 + Nassaus, but by the time my opponent and I had teed off, my sponsors would have lined up at least ten times the original bet in side action.

CHAPTER FOUR

My sponsors would pay me $50 to play the match and give me $10 for each birdie (charging me $5 for bogies). By the time I was 16, I was shooting 66 or 67 regularly and my pockets were bulging with cash. I'd begun skipping school to work on my game. I knew by then that golf would be my life.

Side action also helped me in my first "big" success at the National Junior Jaycee Championship in 1951. In two of the early rounds of the match-play format, I trailed my opponents on the back nine with holes running out.

I tapped into my gambling mode to lift the level of my game. I proposed some side bets, $10 a hole, and promptly staged winning rallies in each match. I seemed to play better with money riding on the line. Some guys are like that.

As my game matured, my hometown sponsors, especially a grand old man named Red Greenway, would take me all over the South to play pre-arranged matches. There were plenty of side bets and a lot of money changed hands. Most of it wound up in Red's, since I proved to be a good "money player."

As I would later learn, what the gamblers in Cedartown were doing with me was no different than what golf gamblers were doing all across the USA. I'm sure that at the very moment I'm writing this somebody's arranging a match between hotshots on which a lot of guys are going to get some money down.

Probably the most famous match of this kind came in the mid-1960s. Titanic Thompson and Ace Darnell in Dallas had lined up a game with Martin Lettunich and his group in El Paso.

Ti had called me to represent the Dallas interests, but I couldn't make it. Instead, young Raymond Floyd, who in those days we called "Junior," took up the mission. Floyd flew out to El Paso for the match at Horizon Hills C.C.

The story goes that when Floyd showed up at the golf course, a Mexican guy came out and took his bag to put on a riding cart. Floyd told the Mexican who he was and what he was doing there, and asked if his opponent had shown up.

"I'm the guy you're looking for," said the golf course employee, who happened to be a Mexican named Lee Trevino.

They got it on in a series of matches over three days. Trevino shot the first 36 holes in something like 65–65 to beat Floyd's 67–66. At the end of the day, while Floyd licked his wounds by playing cards in the 19th hole, Trevino would be washing down the golf carts and tending to matters in the pro shop.

The ironic thing was the Dallas gamblers betting against Trevino were some of his old cronies from Tenison Park. When Trevino left Dallas and moved to El Paso a few years earlier he couldn't putt worth a damn. Obviously he had learned how in the interim.

On the last 9 holes, Raymond Floyd shot 31 to get even on his own money, but the Dallas backers still lost a bunch of money on the match. After the smoke had cleared, Floyd paid Trevino the ultimate compliment. "I left some money back in El Paso," he admitted. "But I ain't going to try to get it back."

Floyd and Trevino would meet again many times in the years ahead. Neither would ever forget their duel in the West Texas sun.

Side Action

Longest Drive in Fairway
(Also called Yardage)

There's no mystery here: the longest tee shot that stays in the fairway wins a side bet of a predetermined amount. "Rocket it and pocket it" is the expression.

The game is an excellent one for players of near-equal ability, however, because the tee shot is so critical on every hole. A good, long drive in the fairway will set up a hole and give a player the opportunity to make par or better.

I've noticed through the years playing in pro-am events and charitable fund-raisers like my own Doug Sanders Celebrity Classic that too many amateur players try to achieve extra distance by swinging from their heels.

The veins in their necks will stand out, their tricep muscles will be bobbing up and down while they stand at address position, and when they swing it's like they try to corkscrew themselves into the ground.

All they accomplish by overswinging and trying to muscle up is to destroy swing tempo. That leads to a whole new set of problems.

The trick to good long drives is to concentrate on making consistent contact, putting the sweet spot of the clubface directly on the ball. A smoother, more relaxed swing produces better distance, believe me. By having a side bet riding on each tee shot, players will learn to improve their driving ability.

Hammer

The golf game Hammer is popular in all parts of the United States and is a favorite of low handicappers. Hammer can be compared with the popular board game backgammon, in that it hinges on a "doubling" device.

A golfer at any point during a hole may call out, "Hammer." The effect is the same as if he used the doubling cube in backgammon: if his opponent accepts the Hammer, the unit value of the bet is immediately doubled and play continues. If the opponent elects not to accept the Hammer, the bet on that hole is over at once, regardless of subsequent play. The loser now has the Hammer, and a new bet begins on the next tee.

For example, let's say Phil and Fred are playing a game of Hammer for $1 a hole. They flip a coin and Fred starts off with the Hammer. Phil tees off and puts his ball in the trees, while Fred strikes his ball straight down the middle.

Fred sees an immediate advantage and calls "Hammer" to Phil. Phil decides to gamble and accepts the Hammer from Fred (the decision to accept the Hammer or to concede must be made immediately), which increases the bet to $2.

The players discover that despite being in the trees, Phil has a direct shot to the green. He hits an iron shot to within six feet of the stick and immediately "Hammers" Fred back. Fred now must concede a $2 bet to Phil or accept the Hammer and continue to play the hole for $4.

Remember: the Hammer must be accepted or rejected immediately, before another shot is made. Whether the Hammer is accepted or rejected, possession of the Hammer changes after every call.

The major appeal of Hammer is all the ebb and flow. Action-oriented players love it. I've seen a strategically called "Hammer" cause many a golfer to bow to pressure. Shots one can routinely execute become more difficult with the added pressure.

My advice is don't try to be a hero. Know your own game and your opponent's game well enough so that you don't go accepting Hammers that you shouldn't. Don't try to be so macho that you accept a Hammer and find yourself having to execute a miracle shot that even Walter Hagen in his prime couldn't have pulled off.

But on the other hand, don't fail to take immediate action if you see an opening present itself. Take a page from the Trini Lopez songbook ("If I Had A Hammer") and hammer your opponents all over this land . . .

Roll 'em

My buddy John Brodie, the great NFL quarterback with the San Francisco 49ers who now plays the PGA Senior Tour, likes to play a game called Roll 'em at the La Quinta C.C. in Palm Springs, California.

The game awards a maximum of five points per hole, one each for low ball, low total, closest to the pin in regulation, sandies and birdies (it's similar to the game Scotch, except for the bet on sandies). If a team gets all five points on a hole, it earns an extra bet.

Roll 'em also features a doubling device as in the game of Hammer. But the doubles (Brodie calls them "Snaps") can be made only twice during a round and only when your team is trailing in overall points.

Snaps can be issued before the opposing team tees off or even when a ball is in the air, but they cannot be made after the ball hits the ground. Unlike Hammer, where the proposition of doubling the bet can be accepted or rejected, Snaps cannot be turned down.

Roll 'em is an action-oriented game that forces teammates to communicate as to when to issue the Snaps.

John told me about a game of Roll 'em where a side bet was proposed to an 18-handicapper. The bet was $10,000 that he couldn't break 111 playing from the tips of the hotel course at La Quinta.

After 15 holes, the player stood at 89. On the par-three 16th hole, he hit the green in regulation but four-putted for a five, pushing his score to 94. On seventeen, he elected to play around a lake instead of carrying it and took an eight for 102.

The 18-handicapper needed eight or better on the final hole to win the bet. He used six strokes to reach the green, and his first putt (the 109th shot) stopped 18 inches short of the hole. It all came down to one putt: if he made it for a 110 he'd win $10,000, but if he missed the putt he'd have 111 and would lose the same amount.

The player addressed his putt three separate times and each time paralysis set in. He froze up as stiff as a block of ice, unable even to draw the putter back. Finally, he looked at the other players (who all had pieces of the action) and pleaded, "Let's make a deal guys. How about if we call the whole thing off?" After some animated discussion and a split decision, one of the members of the group, a guy named Tom Hanson, said, "Sure. Pick it up."

I wanted to mention Brodie's story because of the lesson it teaches. First, the 18-handicapper had no business playing for $10,000. Whether or not he could pay it off isn't the point (if he hangs out in Palm Springs, money's probably not an issue); my point is that everyone who gambles has a pressure point in betting, and his comfort zone was somewhere below ten grand.

Golf is a game that's meant to be enjoyed. If you want to make a small wager here or there, fine. If you want to make a large wager here or there, that's fine too. But don't let your bets take you into the danger zone, where that 18-handicapper found himself. I'm sure he wasn't having much fun standing over that last putt.

The second lesson the story teaches is that sometimes it's better to let a wager lapse than to see it all the way through. Tom Hanson and the others were wise to let the wager go unresolved. If the 18-handicapper had missed the shot there is no telling how long he would have taken to get over it. Money isn't everything, a fact many golfers should keep in mind.

Disaster
(Also Called Bong)

A popular game in the Southwest is played by keeping a side bet on the number of disaster points incurred during the round. The player with the highest total pays the others in the group.

Disaster employs the following scoring system:

Calamity	Penalty Points
Teeing off in front of marker	1
Out of Bounds	1
In a Hazard	1
In the Bunker	1
In the Water	1
Lost Ball	3
Leaving Ball in Trap	3
Leaving Ball in Trap Twice	5
Blasting One Trap to Another	3
Three Putt	3
Four Putt	5
Whiff	5

During the round, players are assessed penalty points for the infractions cited above. At the end of the round, players compare Disaster points. On occasion, a player who has lost the regular bet can recoup some of his losses by having fewer Disaster points.

Keeping tabs on Disaster points is a revealing exercise that will tell you a lot about your game. It will point out strong suits and areas that need work. I'd recommend that you try it at least for a couple of rounds.

Do-Don'ts

Do-Don'ts are popular call bets. A player can call a Do-Don't bet at any time during a round.

Say a player finds an approach shot buried under the lip of a trap guarding the green. If he sees a way to execute the shot, he might call a $5 "Do bet" on hitting the green. Any of his playing partners can then call a "Don't bet," which in essence says he won't be able to get on the green.

Another way to use Do-Don't bets is for a 9-hole score. A player has to shoot his average score or better. A player who averages 40 a side, for example, might say he'll shoot a 39 for a $5 Do and a 38 for a $10 Do. Other players can accept or reject his terms, while creating their own Do-Don't bets.

Do-Don'ts also serve as a scoring device for foursome games. Teams will get $1 a hole if they do shoot par; they will lose $1 a hole if they don't; they will get $1 a hole for each hole they win. They get $2 for the low medal score.

You know, just hearing the name of this game reminds me that in my early days on the PGA Tour I met some attractive ladies in the gallery who'd say that they "Do" and it wasn't until I'd bought them a nice dinner and took them dancing for the evening that they changed their story and said they "Don't."

Fortunately for me, those occasions were pretty rare.

Trash

Some of the most heavy side action in golf rewards players for executing a single shot. These bets, commonly called "Trash," include Greenies, Birdies, Sandies and a host of others. Typically, the action on the first tee will include assigning a unit value for each of these shots.

These games are extremely popular with mid- and high-handicappers, for whom they represent infrequent occurrences.

Perhaps a few definitions are in order:

GREENIES—These are tee shots on par-3 holes won by the member of the group who hits his shot on the green and nearest to the hole. (Note: Some people play that the winner sacrifices his greenie if he three-putts the hole. In that case, the player with the ball next closest to the hole wins the greenie. If only one player hits the green but then three-putts, no greenie is awarded.) Playing for greenies on every hole is growing in popularity among better players.

BIRDIES—These are the things I like best in life. Okay, make that second best.

SANDIES—These are scrambles from out of a greenside trap, where the player saves par by executing one sand shot and one putt. (In most games, a Sandie isn't considered valid unless it saves par. Some players, however, consider a Sandie to be any bunker shot followed by one putt.)

WHALIES—These occur when a player saves par on a hole after being in the water on any shot.

POLIES—These are approach irons from the fairway (second shots on par 4s or third shots on par 5s, that end up within the length of the flagstick or pole (from which the term "Polie" derives). The average flagstick is roughly eight feet long.

STOBBIES—These are approach shots that come to rest within the putter head (5″ or less) of the cup. Of course, since Jack Nicklaus won The Masters with a putter with a 10″ head, and the darn things started selling like gangbusters, a Stobbie ain't what it used to be. But, hey, it's still a pretty fair shot.

CHIP IN—These pay for when you sink a chip shot for a par or better.

HOGAN—In honor of the great Ben Hogan, these are awarded if a player drives in the fairway, hits the green in regulation and makes par or better on the hole.

ARNIE—In honor of Arnold Palmer, these are awarded if a player misses the fairway with his drive but hits the green in regulation and makes par or better.

(John Sorley, one of the veteran caddies at St. Andrews, says the Scottish definition of happiness is "a long walk with your putter." Making a Hogan or an Arnie allows you to do just that.)

CHI-CHI—In honor of super scrambler Chi-Chi Rodriguez, these are awarded if a player misses both the fairway and the green in regulation but still makes par or better on the hole.

APPEARANCE—An appearance is having the honor on the tee after the first hole. Variations of this bet penalize players who play 9 or 18 holes without making an "appearance."

Thirty-Two

The number 32 is one of the most famous in sports. Sandy Koufax, the Dodgers' incomparable lefthander, wore number 32. So did O.J. Simpson of the Buffalo Bills and Jim Brown of the Cleveland Browns.

The number 32 has its place in the game of golf as well. A "Thirty-Two" is a call bet that a player can make against his opponent when he thinks the opponent will three-putt a green. The player calling the "Thirty-Two" is risking 3 to 2 odds that his hunch will be correct.

The person putting has the right to accept or reject the bet. If he accepts the bet, and does indeed three-putt, he owes the player who called the "Thirty-Two" two bets. If the person putting accepts the bet and either one putts or two putts, he wins three units.

Typically, the unit values are determined at the beginning of a round and are less than the regular team or individual bet. For example, if a game is for $5 a hole, the Thirty-Two bets may be $1 each.

But no matter how you set up the action, the Thirty-Twos are thinking man's bets. They are perfect bets for observant players. By that I mean the kind of player who notices when his opponent's concentration is beginning to break. Or the kind of player who can recognize that his opponent is putting from the worst spot on the green (like straight downwhill from above a ridge) and will have difficulty getting down in two.

Since a "Thirty-Two" is something of a slap in the face, players with big egos will likely accept them. Sometimes they'll take bets they shouldn't. Don't you be among that group.

Paul Bunyan

This is one of the "32" series of side bets, so called because a player risks 3 to 2 odds on his opponent's inability to execute a difficult shot. It's probably popular in the Great Lakes states, where Paul and his blue ox, Babe, remain legends.

A Paul Bunyan can be proposed on the tee of a narrow, tree-lined fairway or after a player has hit a drive deep into the woods. Whoever calls the Paul Bunyan is saying his opponent cannot execute the next shot without hitting a tree.

As with most side bets, the Paul Bunyan can be used strategically to give the opponent one more thing to worry about.

A player accepting this "32" bet (in some versions a player must accept this bet) may not elect to play a "safety" to win the bet. He must "Go For It" by taking his normal shot.

As with all the 32 games, Paul Bunyan pays the shotmaker 3 bets if he executes the shot or costs him 2 bets if he's unsuccessful.

Lawrence of Arabia

Another of the "32" series of bets, Lawrence of Arabia is a call bet you can make against your opponent when you think he'll hit his next shot into a sand trap.

The bet is usually called on long par-3 where the green is surrounded by traps. But it can be used on the approach shot to any well-guarded green.

The bet signifies that you don't think your opponent can avoid the sand. You'll risk paying him 3 times the bet if he makes the shot to collect 2 times the bet if he fails to avoid the trap.

As with the Paul Bunyan and other Thirty-Two bets, the opponent must attempt his normal shot.

Davy Jones

Yet another of the popular "32" series of bets, Davy Jones can be invoked whenever water comes into play on a shot. The game is especially popular on newer courses, which often have more water than older tracts, and on courses in the southern states like Florida.

Davy Jones is a call bet that says you don't believe your opponent can make a shot without getting his ball wet.

You're willing to offer 3 to 2 odds to satisfy your curiosity. He gets 3 times the bet for successfully executing the shot, while you get 2 times the bet if he fails to do so.

A variation of the game is called "Splash," wherein every time a player hits one into the drink he must give a new ball to everyone else in the group.

That's a good disciplinary measure for players who have a tendency to try shots they have little chance of executing. "Splash" helps mediocre players improve their course management.

Rabbit

Rabbit is a popular side action bet, with a unit value assigned to the furry little creature. In its most basic form, the game is played like this:

On the first tee, the Rabbit is loose. As soon as a player wins a hole outright, he takes the Rabbit. He keeps the critter until another player wins a hole, at which time the Rabbit again is on the loose. When another hole is won, that player takes the Rabbit. And so on.

The object of the game is to have possession of the Rabbit after the 9th and 18th holes, for which you win a set amount from all the other players in the group.

A variation of the basic game includes adding the Rabbit's legs. For example, if I win the first hole, I have one leg of the Rabbit. If I win another hole, I capture the second leg. Now, I can lose a hole and still have one leg, which at the end of 9 holes is worth one bet.

Another way to pay off on Rabbit is to calculate the number of holes each player keeps the Rabbit (or the Rabbit's legs) during a round, with a set amount awarded per hole. That's similar to the Indy 500, which pays a driver an amount for each lap he leads the race, regardless of where he finishes.

The high-stakes version of Rabbit calls for the bet to be doubled each time the Rabbit gets caught. The more turnovers in possession during a round, the larger the pot.

My buddy Charlie Owens, the PGA Senior Tour player, likes to play a variation of Rabbit called "Squirrel." The rules are the same, but to win the Squirrel a person has to shoot a birdie.

The Bogey Game

Before anyone had heard of "The Merry Mex," a term I happened to coin at the '68 U.S. Open, Lee Trevino and his buddies at Tenison Park in Dallas were playing a side game they called "The Bogey Game."

It worked like this: whoever shot a bogey immediately owed the other players in the group $5. Plus the figurative clock started running, and he owed another $5 for each hole his opponents played until *they* made a bogey.

So if you bogied number one and another member of the group played a bogey-less front side, you'd owe him $45 ($5 for the original bogey plus $40 for the next eight holes). And that didn't include the others in the group.

Of course, as soon as the others bogey they owe you $5 plus another $5 for the holes you can run off at par or better.

It may sound confusing, but it's a top-notch game for top-notch players.

I know one thing, for sure. As good a money player as Trevino is, I'm glad I grew up in Cedartown, Georgia, and not Dallas, Texas.

Honest John

Honest John is the name of a popular side bet in which each player guesses what he will shoot before the round begins. The players write their predicted score on a slip of paper, and all the slips are placed in an envelope and sealed.

Everyone puts a specified amount into a pot and if a player hits his score on the nose, he wins. (If two or more players hit the right number, the pot is split accordingly.)

The rules stipulate that if you shoot a double bogey or higher on either 17 or 18, you cannot win the game. This prevents a player from throwing off strokes at the end to win the bet.

The real appeal of Honest John is that it's a side bet. Players want to win the pot, of course, but not if it means jeopardizing a larger bet to do so. Strategy comes into play on the finishing holes, since playing partners can't know for sure who's trying to save—or add—strokes.

Hold The Box

Jim Cochran, one of the PGA Senior Tour members who plays out of St. Louis, likes to play a side bet that concerns holding honors on the tee.

Before the round begins, teams flip a coin to see who has the honors on the first hole. The object of the game is to keep the honors for a predetermined number of holes, usually six or nine. If the team holds the box, the losing team pays a set amount agreed upon before the coin flip.

I've always believed too much side action can be a distraction during a round. Hold The Box, though, is easy to manage and is a lot of fun, especially because if you win this bet it means you've probably won the other bets as well.

Humility

This a game popular with teenagers, since they're world class at giving each other the rag.

The way it works is that as soon as you lose a hole, you have to carry your opponent's bag until you win a hole back.

As hung-up as teenagers can be on appearances—I know I was a cocky so-and-so from the time I was 13—it can be a humbling experience to be seen having to tote another player's bags for several holes.

The game is especially damaging to reputations when played on courses that are flat and wide open, where views from several fairways over are unobstructed.

Humility can make your day—or ruin it.

Gimme The Putt

This side bet is particularly prized by good putters. The game primarily involves wagering on putts in the knee-knocker range from two to five feet.

A player can call "Gimme The Putt" at any time, and his opponent must either concede it or tell him to putt out.

If the putt isn't conceded, a new bet is created for that putt only. For example, suppose Jim and Bob are playing for $5 a hole, and after Bob has made a bogey Jim asks Bob to concede a 4-foot putt for par. Bob refuses and tells Jim to putt it.

If Jim sinks that putt he wins the hole, plus the new bet, or $10 total. If Jim misses the putt, he ties the hole and loses the new bet, or a $5 loss.

Long Holes

This is a game that's popular in Colorado and other Rocky Mountain states where you can hit the ball nine miles.

Long Holes is an uncomplicated bet that rewards the player who wins the longest holes. A standard low ball format is used, but when a player wins a hole, instead of being 1-up he is ahead by the yardage of the hole.

Say in a 9-hole match, player A wins holes that measure 350, 450 and 500 yards (total: 1300 yards), player B wins holes that measure 200 and 400 yards (total: 600 yards) and four holes are halved.

Player A would win the match by 700 units. At a penny a yard that comes to $7.00; but at a nickel a yard he's out $35.00 and so on.

There's no question this game favors the big hitters like a Greg Norman or an Andy Bean, but you still have to score well to win.

One word to the wise: be sure to pay attention when the terms are established, because this bet can get expensive in a hurry.

Strip Golf

This game illustrates not only that golfers do crazy things, but if they don't have cash they'll find other things to wager.

In the early 1960s, two students at the University of Texas wanted to gamble at golf but neither one had any cash. No problem. They bet their articles of clothing, in effect creating a game of strip golf.

The kid named Muse (no one recalls his first name) lost his shirt, literally, on the front nine. On the back side, his shoes, socks and pants followed. Finally, on the 17th green, he missed a putt and lost his jockey shorts.

The winner of the match, a guy named George Marsh, Jr., took everything from Muse except his car keys. Muse then had to run buck naked from the 18th tee to the parking lot. He had to run past the clubhouse and the swimming pool en route, and a bunch of startled females (this was long before the "streaking" fad) caught Muse in full swing, er, stride.

I must say I've heard of beating the pants off your opponent—but never before like this.

The Tournament Trail

When you've played tournament golf as long as I have, you get used to a variety of formats and rules. Over the past 40 years, I've played in practically every kind of tournament imaginable: match play, medal play, mixed foursome, Scotch foursomes, best-ball, pro-am—you name it.

I've played tournament golf ever since 1945, when I entered a caddie tournament at the 9-hole public course in my hometown. I was lucky enough to win that one, which gave me a feeling of confidence that I could one day make a name for myself in golf.

My education as a tournament player accelerated sharply in 1951, when I went to Durham, North Carolina, and won the National Junior Jaycee Championship. That win more than anything else established the credentials I needed to be offered a golf scholarship to the University of Florida.

At Gainesville I was the captain of some pretty good Gator teams that also included future pros like Dave Ragan and Dan Sikes. After us came a host of PGA players from Bob Murphy to Andy Bean to Andy North.

I must admit that college and Doug Sanders didn't exactly go hand-in-hand. It was more like hand in golf glove. I majored in partying and minored in women (or was it vice versa?) and spent so much time at the golf course, as opposed to going to class, that I never did pick up my degree.

Although it didn't seem to matter much at the time, as the years have passed I've come to regret not finishing my degree requirements. It's probably one of the reasons I have become so involved with my college scholarship program for junior players worldwide. We can't stress the importance of education enough to our children.

Anyway, my big breakthrough came at the Canadian Open in July 1956. I was still an amateur at the time, but I fashioned four consecutive rounds in the 60s and tied Dow Finsterwald with a 72-hole score of 273. On the first hole of the sudden-death playoff, Dow got into trouble and made bogey, and I found myself the winner of one of the most prestigious titles in golf.

Until collegian Scott Verplank came along in July 1985 and won the Western Open in a playoff with Jim Thorpe, no amateur had won a tournament on the professional circuit since my magnificent week in Montreal.

I don't want to say that my performance in the Canadian Open had anything to do with my meeting on the eve of the first round an attractive English lady who told me that if I won the tournament she'd take care of me for a night. But I don't remember squeezing the handsome Seagram's trophy, given to the Canadian Open winner each year, any tighter than I squeezed her that Sunday night after the tournament was over.

As I mentioned, my first win came in a playoff with Dow Finsterwald, and one of my most unforgettable PGA wins came in a playoff ten years later at the Bob Hope Desert Classic. This time I beat one of Dow's best buddies, a fellow named Arnold Palmer.

Palmer loved playing the Bob Hope (we all did, for that matter) and he loved playing desert courses where he could muscle the ball through the thin air. As a result, playing a five-day, 90-hole tournament was tailor made for his game. Arnie's affinity for the event was reflected in the fact he won the Hope Classic five times, including in 1973 for his 61st (and last) Tour win.

In 1966, though, I scratched and clawed my way into a playoff with The King. I should point out it was early in the year and I was being more or less faithful to my New Year's resolution to train hard and take my game seriously. Which meant, for example, that I was drinking orange juice for breakfast, not screwdrivers.

Anyway, after Bob Hope congratulated us both and cracked a few one-liners for the national TV audience, the playoff began. We started on a par-3 hole, and I knew damn well I didn't want the playoff to last till we got to a par-5 because if it did, Palmer would hitch up his trousers, sniff once or twice and bust a big drive and fairway wood to close me out.

So I called on a little gamesmanship to try and get the upper hand. Before we teed off, and in front of the small gallery that had raced back to the tee, I turned to The King and said, "Arnie, let's play winner take all. What do you say?"

First-place in the Hope was worth about $15,000, and second-place paid $8,000. There were plenty of precedents where PGA players that found themselves in playoffs agreed to split the money for first and second place, regardless of the outcome. Never mind what the Monday headlines or the money-winning lists said, a lot of deals were cut.

But here I was, willing to gamble the entire $23,000 on one hole. Against the greatest golfer in the world! Was my alligator mouth overloading my canary ass once again?

The surprising thing, though, was that Arnie didn't take my bet. He shot me a quizzical look, like he thought I was joking. But what I read into his expression was indecision. The boldest player I ever saw appeared to me to be having doubts. Right then, I knew I had to be an 8-5 favorite to win the hole. And sure enough, that surge of confidence helped me hit a 7-iron to 18 feet of the cup and drill my birdie putt into the back of the hole. The next day, the headline in Los Angeles paper read: "Sanders Two, Palmer's Through."

Palmer wasn't through, of course, not by a long shot. But for one day, I had the upper hand on the best player in the game. Even if it took a little gamesmanship to get there.

Later that same year, a bizarre occurrence took place at the Pensacola Open, which for me was like the Bob Hope Classic was for Arnie. I loved playing at Pensacola. I loved the course, the Pensacola C.C., and I loved the fact that so many of my old friends from Georgia and Florida showed up to watch me play.

I'd already won the Pensacola Open in 1962 and again in 1965, when I beat Jack Nicklaus in a playoff. As defending champion in 1966, I liked my chances to win for a third time. I especially liked them after I started 63-67 for a 130 total and a four-stroke lead after 36 holes.

But a funny thing happened to me on the way to the official scorer's tent, although it wasn't funny at the time. We had finished the second round on the ninth green—it was soon after the PGA fields had expanded and play started on both the first and tenth tees—and there was no place to sit down and go over your and your playing partners' scorecards.

Instead, you had to hoof it over to the 18th green, where the scorer's tent was set up. As it turned out, on the way over there I was besieged by autograph seekers. Since it's always been my nature to try and please everyone, I was only too happy to oblige.

One elderly lady told me she'd been trying to get my autograph for several years. She handed me a sheet of paper to sign, and I placed it on top of my scorecard. I wrote a little message and signed "Doug Sanders." Subconsciously, I guess, I must have thought I had signed my scorecard. That wasn't the case, however, and I negligently turned the scorecard in without it having my John Hancock on it.

The next thing I know word came down from the PGA that I had been disqualified. Their decision caused a big stink—made mostly by me—and it cost me a $10,000 check for first-place.

But it served to teach me an important lesson about tournament golf: it ain't over until the scorecards are verified to make sure all the i's are dotted and the t's are crossed.

And that's true for everybody, even if you're Doug Sanders and you ain't got no i's or t's in your name.

Tournament Games

Scrambles

"Scramble" is one of those golf terms that has several meanings and uses. Golfers frequently use the word to mean they extracted themselves from a precarious situation. "I really scrambled on that hole," you'll hear a golfer say after he's turned a potential disaster into a par.

Used in that sense, scramble is synonymous with another golf term, "up and down." The player who misses a high number of greens but saves par on the holes will say he "scrambled" well.

In tournament golf or gambling golf, however, Scramble generally refers to a format for play. A Scramble involves a group (often a foursome or fivesome) that plays a tournament (18 or 36 holes and occasionally 54 holes). Teams are usually structured with low-, medium- and high-handicappers, to balance the field.

The basic Scramble format calls for all players in the group to hit drives on the hole. The teammates confer and select the best drive (the choice is usually clearcut) and from that spot they all hit second shots. Again they choose the best second ball to play a third shot, and so on until the ball is in the cup. This format is known as a Florida Scramble.

A variation on the Florida Scramble format is to make mandatory the use of each player's drive on one, two, or even three holes during the round. This adds an extra element of strategy to the game and also eliminates having one skillful player dictating a team's fortunes.

When you have to use one of the drives of all players, often the best way to handle the decision is to elect to play the first reasonably good drive of the team's worst player. The last thing a team wants to do is to keep the onus on the high-handicapper until late in the round and then recoil in shock when he tops or skulls a drive into a hazard or out-of-bounds. It's a good idea to take the pressure off high-handicappers as soon as possible.

Another variation of the scramble, popular at the golfing hotbed of Myrtle Beach, South Carolina, is to use a shotgun start and play the first hole as a practice hole. The warmup hole then serves as the 18th hole of their official round. This format relieves some of the "first hole jitters" that are common in tournaments and gives the players 19 holes for their money—sort of a baker's dozen.

Best Ball
(Best 2 Balls, Best 3 Balls)

Many of the tournaments played at country clubs or publinx courses are set up around foursomes, and one of the most common formats is the Best Ball tournament.

In these events a foursome plays the hole, adjusts for their handicaps, then posts a lowest score. One potential problem with the format is that players who aren't having their best days tend to lose concentration. They figure someone else in the group will "pick them up."

For that reason, there are different formats for Best Ball competitions that will keep the players more involved in the game. One is a Best Three Balls format, where you throw out one score on the hole and post the lowest three. Another is a Best Two Balls format, where you throw out two scores and post the other two.

In my opinion, the most competitive of all these variations is Three Best Balls. That keeps everyone involved in the game, and you'll be surprised how high the scores will be in relation to par. You'll see much higher scores than in Best Two Balls.

Long and Short

Many golfers have one-dimension games. Some are good ballstrikers but are erratic around the greens. Others tend to spray their woods and iron shots, but putt, chip and pitch with a deft touch.

This event melds those types of talent. One player hits the balls to within 100 yards of the green, at which point the other player takes over and finishes out the hole.

This is a fun game for foursomes to play. Adjustments can be made as to where the short game player takes over. You might want to play from 50 yards in.

Players who've tried long and short give it high marks for the interaction and the tag-team factor.

Quota Systems

Quota systems are popular in many parts of the country, especially the Upper Midwest around Chicago and Milwaukee. They keep all players involved in every shot and every hole, because everything counts.

A basic quota system works like this:

Double Bogey (or higher)	0 points
Bogey	1 point
Par	2 points
Birdie	3 points
Eagle	4 points

The game can be played using gross scores on each hole or net scores adjusted to handicap.

The foursome plays and each member totals up points.

The payoff can be set in several ways:

1. A fixed amount paid by the other golfers to the player with the highest total (good shots are rewarded with more points);
2. A fixed amount paid by the player with the lowest total to the other golfers.
3. A fixed amount for the difference in the total points between each player.

Hypothetically, Player A scores 30 points, Player B 23 points, Player C 20 points and Player D 18 points. Assuming a 50 cents game per point, using the third example the payoffs would be as follows:

PLAYER A—Wins $14.50
PLAYER B—Wins $.50
PLAYER C—Loses $5.50
PLAYER D—Loses $9.50

Under that system, the sum total will always be zero, with the total winnings and total losings canceling each other out.

Points can be structured to reward good shots and penalize bad ones. In the example above, the system was a simple 1,2,3,4 for bogies, pars, birdies, and eagles. But good shots could be rewarded by keeping bogies at 1 point and raising pars to 3, birdies to 6, and eagles to 9. Or bad shots could be penalized by subtracting 2 points for double bogies and 5 points for triple bogies.

Any modification to the standard system should be made with care. The PGA Tour used a quota system (The Stableford) at The International at Castle Pines, Colorado, in 1986 and created a hornet's nest among the players who objected to the scoring system of minus points for bogeys or higher, and no points for pars.

Quota systems are testimony that you can't please everyone all the time—but you still ought to try.

Blind Holes

Why do people enjoy bingo, lotteries, and raffles so much? Because of the suspense. You never know when you're number might be picked.

So it is with Blind Hole tournaments, where the winning score is determined by an individual or team's play on 9 holes.

Only no one knows which 9 holes are in play until after the last group has teed off. Players have no knowledge of which holes count until they have finished play.

The attractive feature of this game is that nearly every individual or team has at least 9 good holes on their card, so they generally feel they have a chance to win. That spurs a concerted effort on everyone's part.

Contrast that with other tournaments where if an individual falls apart and has no chance to win, his actions and manners can be a disruptive influence on others in his group—players who have a chance to win.

We've all seen players fly off the handle and start throwing clubs, cussing, making the game miserable for others in the group. Blind Holes eliminates many problems of that nature, since players can put a 7 or an 8 behind them and go on to the next hole.

The bad holes can be put behind you—unless a number of those holes show up in the "draw."

Six-Six-Six

Six-Six-Six is a format for tournament play that gets its name from the fact that within an 18-hole round, three separate formats are used for six holes each.

On the first six holes, two-man teams post a score of their best ball. On the second six holes, the teammates hit alternate shots to post a medal score. On the final six holes, teams play a two-man scramble, where both players hit each shot and then select the best one.

It makes for a fun afternoon and a variety of shotmaking and decision-making. Personally, I wish more club pros would consider having a Six-Six-Six tournament for their members.

As I've tried to emphasize, there are many different ways to enjoy golf. Six-Six-Six blends three popular formats into one game, and club members who've tried it tell me it makes for a great tournament. As the old TV commercial used to say: "Try it...you'll like it."

Match vs. Par

This is a fun tournament game that pits a player against Old Man Par.

It works like this: players use their full handicaps where they fall on the card and square off with par.

The scoring in this game is on a hole-by-hole basis. If on the par-4 first hole, a person shoots a natural 6 and receives a stroke for a net 5, he is 1-down to par.

The winner of the tournament is the player who is the most holes "Up" on par after the round.

Games like this enable the mid- to high-handicappers to have incentives on each hole and put bad holes behind them.

Drop Out

This game is similar to Match vs. Par. Again, each player is allowed his full handicap, and the strokes are taken as they fall on the card.

Everyone is playing against par and remains in the contest until he loses a hole to par. At that point he's eliminated from the contest.

As in the game of Horserace, the object of the game is survival. The winner of Drop Out is the player who completes the most holes before losing one to Old Man Par.

Call Shot

This is a game popular with foursomes. Its unique quality is that frequently you may play your partner's ball, and he may play yours.

After tee shots are hit, partners decide who they want to hit the second shots—regardless of who hit the respective drives.

The shots must be evenly distributed throughout the play of each hole. The game is similar to a Scotch, except shots are not necessarily alternated and two balls are played through to the hole.

Call Shot is generally played for low ball and low total, so scores count on every shot.

The game is designed to accentuate the varied abilities of the team members. If one teammate is skilled at sand shots, he may be assigned to hit out of all the bunkers. Others might have an advantage with long or medium irons that would dictate their involvement on specific shots.

Scotch and Modified Scotch

Scotch and Modified Scotch are popular formats for tournament play, especially for mixed couples events.

In a pure Scotch event, partners alternate on every shot. One drives, the other hits second, and play reverts back and forth until the entire round (not just one hole) is completed.

In a Modified Scotch event, both partners tee off and select which ball they wish to play. The partner whose ball *was not* selected hits the second shot, and the players alternate until the hole is completed. The Modified Scotch format adds an element of strategy to the proceedings.

Personally, I have nothing against Scotch, but I prefer Gin.

Flag Day

In this popular tournament game, each player is given a small flag to carry around. He sticks it in the ground at the exact spot where his ball lies after he has taken the number of strokes equal to par plus his handicap. (A 15-handicapper playing a par 70 course would get to hit 85 shots, for example.)

Whoever carries his flag farthest around the course wins the flag tournament. The overall winner usually plants his flag on the 19th or

20th hole, and if anyone proceeds much farther it may be prudent to have his handicap adjusted.

Many clubs, incidentally, award prizes to everyone who holes out on the 18th green within their allotted number of strokes.

One point I'd like to stress is that miniature U.S. flags should never be used as Flag Day markers, not even on the Fourth of July.

I sure as hell don't want to see Old Glory sitting in a divot somewhere. Do you?

The Long and Short of Putting

Want to know the biggest difference between scratch golfers and professionals? That's easy. It's the same difference between the low handicappers and the scratch golfers: the short game.

Chipping, pitching, and putting. Especially putting, since you have to putt at least once on virtually every hole.

Within 50 feet of the cup is where pros save the strokes that the amateurs have to write down on their cards. We can execute the tricky chips and pitches from the trouble spots around the green. We can step into a bunker and, given a decent lie, expect to hit everything within two or three feet. Often we twist our feet into the sand to anchor ourselves with the expectation we are going to *sink* the shot.

Not that we necessarily do, mind you, but we know we have a chance. We have hit these shots so many times and learned so much about how to execute short game situations, that we are adept at boiling three shots into two. At getting up and down.

Pros always expect to have 30 putts or less during a round. Any more than that and we know to look for our names on the tournament scoreboard from the bottom up, not from the top down. But not a whole lot of amateurs, even the real good ones, handle the putter with such deftness. Rounds with fewer than 30 putts for them are more the exception than the rule.

I think it's safe to say that the average golfer—the guy who carries a handicap between 10 and 20—could probably shave three to four strokes a round off his score by concentrating on his putting stroke. He'd eliminate some unnecessary three-putt greens, for one thing, and he'd also have more one-putt greens than he might imagine.

But how often do you actually see anyone working on his putting stroke? It's very rare. Instead, you see guys down at the practice range hitting bucket after bucket of balls to groove their swing. From the standpoint of scoring, they'd be much better off spending that time at the practice green, grooving their putting stroke.

Have you ever wondered why it's generally only the best players at your club that you see out practicing on the putting green? Think about that for a while. If you're interested in scoring, and most golfers who gamble are, I'd say you'd be better off to spend 15 minutes on the practice green than 30 minutes on the practice tee. Of course, if you warm up in the manner I suggested several chapters back, you'll do both before you play.

Putting is an individualistic thing, meaning there's no "right" way to do it. Putters have come in all styles, from Palmer's knocked-knees to Nicklaus' closed stance to Gary Player's little jab at the ball.

Some great putters have used their wrists to putt, some great ones have used only their arms and shoulders and some have used a combination of the two. Whatever works for you is whatever's right.

I know all about doing something your own way, of course. My golf swing has been called one-of-a-kind ever since I became a nationally known player in the mid-1950s. The tag, "Doug Sanders could swing inside a telephone booth," was put on me by a sportswriter from Detroit who watched me win the Western Open in 1958. The tag has stuck ever since.

I know my way of hitting the golf ball isn't a method that many pros would teach, but they probably should. It might not look pretty, but it's effective. Anyway, as I've often said, "Show me a man with a pretty swing, and I'll show you a man I can eat alive."

My telephone-booth swing enabled me to hit a lower, straighter, and more controlled ball than a lot of the other guys. About the only thing I lacked was enough distance to pummel the par-5s the way Arnie and Jack did. But a man couldn't win 20 tournaments without owning a grooved swing that he could rely on. Nor could he stand up to the suffocating pressure on Sunday afternoon without a reliable putting stroke.

I've always believed that a golfer faces the most pressure on the putting surface. Virtually every putt is a "must" putt, especially those six-to-eight footers you need to save par.

Conversely, there are very few "must" shots you have to play from the tee or the fairway, or even the rough. You can generally play several types of drives or approach shots and expect to have some margin for error.

Maybe the 12th tee at Augusta National is an exception. You're standing up there staring down at Rae's Creek. You can tell from the trees that the wind's swirling and you're trying to hit a green no deeper than the feelings of a call girl.

That one "must" shot has sunk the hopes of a lot of players who could see themselves in that famous Masters green jacket, shaking hands with Bobby Jones and Clifford Roberts, or Hord Hardin, who handles the ceremonies now that those two great gentlemen are deceased.

Successful putting is a combination of having a repeatable stroke and a confident attitude on the greens. It's like a loop: the confidence comes from sinking putts and sinking putts comes from having a repeatable stroke.

Probably the best putter the world of golf has seen in the past decade was Tom Watson. I say *was*, because beginning in 1984 or thereabouts, Watson lost some of his confidence on the greens. Those big putts he'd been making for years stopped falling. And as his average putts per round started to rise, his confidence naturally started to sink. He stopped being the aggressive putter he'd always been and became somewhat tentative with his stroke.

Though Watson was hitting the ball with authority from tee-to-green, he went through a long dry spell at the winner's circle.

The exact same thing happened to Arnold Palmer, the King. By the late 1960s and the early 1970s, Palmer was hitting the ball better than he ever had, which was damn good.

But the magic wand he'd waved during the late '50s and early '60s started playing tricks on him. He lost confidence in his stroke and began a long period of experimentation with different putters and strokes, never again quite finding his touch.

In his prime, though, Arnie probably made more big putts than anyone who ever played. With the exception of Jack Nicklaus, that is.

Some players on the PGA Tour—regulars and seniors—change putters about as often as they change shirts. They're always looking for something to give them an edge. If not a real edge, then an imagined one that boosts their confidence.

I'm not one who believes that changing putters is going to change your luck. I'm from the school that holds that the answer lies not with the putter, but with the guy making the stroke.

That's why I still use a putter I started using 25 years ago. It's a cut-down putter from the Doug Sanders' First Flight clubs, about eight-inches or so shorter than the average putter. I started using a shorter putter back in my great days of partying because it was closer to the ground. I figured if I bent down and fell over, I didn't have too far to go.

The shorter putter gave me greater feeling of control on the greens. It also helped me make all the alimony payments, so I figured I should keep it around. I *know* my ex-wives liked that putter.

Naturally over the 25 years we've been together the putter has seen some wear and tear. Once in awhile some trees would jump out and hit it. And on a few occasions, it's spent time in other people's bags. But as soon as I'd see a friend make a putt with it, I'd demand that they give it back.

Within the last year, a lot of the guys on the Senior Tour have gone to the long putter Charlie Owens uses. They've seen him go from being one of the worst putters on the Tour to one of the best. So several of them are trying it as well. Personally, I don't see how a long putter could help your stroke any more than two Bloody Marys.

One of the best putters I've ever seen was George Low. He had an unorthodox method of using his wrists to impart sidespin on the ball, literally "hooking" his putts into the hole.

Billy Casper is another great putter, a fellow who when he got hot was unstoppable. When he won the U.S. Open at Winged Foot in 1959, Casper handled the greens, which were slicker than a baby's bottom, in something like 112 putts. That might have been the single greatest putting performance ever.

Bob Charles, the New Zealander, also belongs on any list of great putters. His stroke is "low and slow and on the inside." I suppose he has to be a great putter to compensate for setting up on the wrong side of the ball.

But if I had to pick one player to make one 20-footer for the keys to the kingdom, it would have to be Jack Nicklaus, especially on fast greens. He's won 20 major titles on the fastest greens we play. When you think of Jack, your first thought is probably about his power, but the secret to his success is that priceless putting stroke. And his ability to "will" the ball into the hole.

If you saw the telecast of the '86 Masters you know what I mean. By the time he arrived at the 17th green, he'd already taken the club out of Seve Ballesteros' hands and he was going to strangle the rest of the field. The Golden Bear had a 10-footer for birdie and you could tell from the look in his eyes there was absolutely no way he would miss.

Once the putt started rolling, Jack starting walking after it. He'd already made up his mind that putt was falling. Period, new paragraph.

There are a few things you must do on your putts. Your hands should work in concert, neither one dominating the stroke. The putter should be accelerating, not decelerating, as you make contact with the ball. The putterhead should follow through down the target line.

But that's basically about it. You can stand erect, squat down, hunch your shoulders, stick out your rump—do whatever you please.

Hell, you can even cross your hands. I've seen some excellent players—from Bruce Lietzke and Bernhard Langer to Charlie Owens—who putt extremely well with a cross-hand stroke.

Of course, my buddy Orville Moody putts cross-handed, and Old

Sarge can't putt a lick. In fact, he sometimes uses two putters during a round, one for the short putts and one for the long ones. When he has a medium-range putt, say a 15-or 20-footer, he's between clubs. I've seen his caddy try to give him one putter only to have Sarge insist on the other one.

Still, Orville Moody won himself a U.S. Open championship, which is something I was never able to do, though I came close several times. So I shouldn't talk about the man's putting.

Putting plays a critical role in golf gambling, of course. Many of the games hinge on scoring, and that often means who sinks the big putt.

Sandies aren't sandies without a one-putt and in some games greenies aren't greenies. You don't make birdies with two putts, unless it's a par-5 hole and you're on in two. The name of the game is scoring. It's not how, but how many.

Anyone who gambles knows the real nut-cutting in golf takes place on the greens. The guys who collect the green stuff are the guys who hammer in the 8- and 10-footers all day long.

It's amazing the number of people I meet along the trail of the PGA Senior Tour who extend their condolences to me for missing that short putt on the last hole of the 1970 British Open at St. Andrews.

I can still see it happen as if it were yesterday. I'm standing there on the 18th green in front of that the magnificent clubhouse of the Royal and Ancient Golf Club, the mecca of golf. The green is ringed with all those Scottish golf fans pulling for me to sink my putt of roughly 30 inches to win golf's most historic prize.

If I make it, I win my first "major" title (although I personally considered each of my 20 PGA Tour wins to be major ones). If I miss it, Jack Nicklaus ties me for first place, forcing a playoff.

I carefully lined up my putt and was about to take the putter back when I noticed a tiny pebble in my line to the cup. I stepped away with my left foot, keeping my right foot anchored, and brushed away the pebble that the harsh afternoon wind had blown into my line.

Then I readdressed the ball, incorrectly I later realized, and hit the ball with the heel of the putter, pushing it an inch outside the cup to the right. In the stunned silence that ensued, I tapped in the comebacker for a bogey five and walked to the scorer's tent, my whole body in utter shock.

The next day, Nicklaus birdied the same 18th hole to beat me by one stroke in an 18-hole playoff.

I've thought about that 30-inch putt many times through the years, though at first I couldn't bear to see pictures of it on TV replays. Nor could I read accounts of the tournament and what had happened.

But I've mellowed through the years and come to terms with the biggest disappointment of my career. After all, I played pretty good that week, and it took the greatest player in the history of the game to beat me. And I know in my heart of hearts, that if I had to do it all over I'd do it the same way, including stepping away before I made my stroke.

Only this time I'd make that rascal.

Putting Games

Snake
(Also Known as Angel or Barracuda)

Snake is the quintessential putting game in golf. It rewards consistency and concentration on the greens and penalizes players who tend
to succumb to pressure. Which, at one time or the other, is everyone
who ever played the game.

In the most basic form of Snake, the last player to three-putt a
green owes the other players one unit of a bet (whatever is agreed
upon). Three-putting a green on the front side generally is no cause
for alarm, but by the 14th or 15th hole, players start anticipating who
will have to pay off.

The most popular form of Snake is played with carryovers, where
each three-putt during a round is added to a cumulative total. If a

three-putt on the 16th green is the last of the day and the fifth three-putt within the group, the offender owes each of the others in the group five units.

For the average player, the two methods of Snake described above can be a lot of fun. Some players like to hiss when a playing partner three-putts and in some groups a rubber snake is passed around and must be hung from the offender's bag until someone else three-putts. Whoever gets stuck with the Snake at the end of a round has to keep up with it until the next game.

Howard Garrett, Ian Johnston, and a group of their buddies at the Lakewood C.C. in Dallas regularly play the same game, but they call it Angel instead of Snake. That's because they were playing one day and as they neared the last hole Ian had a testy short putt to avoid being stuck with the Snake. He prepared to putt, but just before striking the ball he paused and looked up at the other players in his group. "They looked like the Angels of Death," Ian said. "So we immediately changed the name of the game to Angel."

In other parts of the country golfers call the same three-putt game Barracuda. When a player three putts, his playing partners in unison chant " 'cuda, 'cuda."

It's important to remember that in some games when a player uses his putter from off the green, the shot is counted as a pitch or chip, not a putt. But the more popular version holds that any time you pull out the putter, you are putting and therefore eligible for the Snake. The interpretation should be established at the first tee to eliminate the possibility of a misunderstanding later in the round.

High-rollers, meanwhile, play Snake where each three-putt not only carries over, but doubles the unit amount. In the example above, where the three-putt on 16 was the fifth and final one of the day, the offender would owe every other player 16 units (1,2,4,8,16). You need to know what you're doing when this form of Snake is proposed, because a good putter might three-putt several greens on purpose just to get the stakes up and then wait to see who has to pay him later after a three-putt.

I can tell you from experience that playing Snake with carryovers and doubles isn't for the faint of heart or thin of wallet. Some serious money almost always changes hands. As a more moderate game, let me suggest Reno Putts, which draws its name from that mecca for golf action and other games, Reno, Nevada.

Reno Putts

Reno Putts sounds like it could be the name of a parking garage attendant in midtown Manhattan. But, in fact, it's the name of a putting game popular in the desert city of Reno, Nevada.

The way the game is played is this: at the beginning of the round, a unit value is assigned to each putt. At the end of the round, putts

are added and players settle among themselves. The player who needed only 25 putts wins 5 units from the player with 30 putts, and so on, using a simple calculation of putts per player.

A second calculation is made regarding three putts. Each player is allowed two per round, but if he three-putts 3 times he owes the other players five units each. And every additional three-putt thereafter costs him five more units to every player.

This game, too, can be costly for a guy with a balky putter. My old buddy George Bayer told me that he was playing in Reno once when the putting champion of Sacramento rolled into town looking for some action. He'd heard about the game and figured he could clean up.

They got up a game with a package of bets that included sizable terms for Reno Putts. Well, it seems the Californian who was known for his putting prowess back in Sacramento couldn't read the breaks in the Reno greens at all. And on top of that he couldn't figure the speed much better.

The California Kid three-putted the first couple of holes and then he got flustered. By the back nine, Bayer and the boys were into him pretty good. They'd taken all his money, and were working on the guy's wheels. Bayer said they never saw the Sacramento chumpion around Reno after that.

Stymies

Stymies is a putting game that tests both a golfer's skill and strategic thinking. It takes its name from the Stymie, the blocking of one ball by another.

For years, the rules of golf did not permit balls to be spotted and removed from the green. Before golfers were allowed to mark their balls, they occasionally would find themselves blocked or impeded from the hole by an opponent's ball. To have a chance of sinking their shot, players would have to execute the "stymie" shot, taking a lofted club and pitching their ball over the opponent's ball towards the cup.

In 1930, the year he won the Grand Slam, Bobby Jones won one of his matches in the British Amateur on the first playoff hole by leaving his opponent, Cyril Tolley, stymied. Jones reached the par-4 hole in two strokes, while Tolley, the defending champion, needed three to get on. Jones stroked his third shot just inches from the hole, but effectively blocked Tolley's chance to make a putt for par.

Another famous stymie came at the 1938 PGA semifinal match between Sam Snead and Jimmy Hines. After both men hit approach shots to the 14th green, Snead left his birdie putt short of the hole, but directly between Hines' ball and the cup. Hines promptly took out a 9-iron and chipped his ball into the hole for a birdie. Incredibly, however, Hines' ball grazed Snead's as it flew past and sent Snead's ball rolling into the cup as well. Since Snead hadn't struck the ball, he was also credited with a birdie. The good fortune gave him the momentum to pull out a 1-up victory.

Enough golf history: the putting game Stymies is played on the practice green, typically by two or three players, occasionally by more. The game can be nine holes or 18 holes, often depending on your course's practice green.

Most putts are attempted from 20 feet or beyond. The object is to take the fewest number of putts.

Strategy comes into play because of the following rules:

1. No balls are marked. Instead they are left on the green until the player farthest from the hole has putted.
2. Your ball may not make contact with another player's ball. If it does, you lose the hole and owe one unit value to all other players. You also have to putt last on the next hole.

The rules give the advantage to the putter that goes first. You either want to sink your putt or leave it directly in front of the cup. A good lag putt can effectively "Stymie" your opponents.

Putter Length

Putter Length isn't a gambling game per se, though it can be played in conjunction with Snake or Reno Putts. It's a good game to try on the practice green for starters. Some players incorporate it into a regular round.

Putter Length is simple: wherever your first (lag) putt comes to rest, you mark the spot and then measure one putter length away from the hole. Since most putters are roughly 36 inches long, the game adds about three feet to second putts. That makes it a terrific putting drill.

I know one thing: I might have a chance against Charlie Owens at this game, because he's the guy who introduced the putter that's nearly five feet long.

Horseshoes

Horseshoes is a fun putting game to play on the practice green.

The game is played to 21 points. To start, the players (two or more, but two is ideal) establish the sequence for hitting. Each player gets two putts at the hole. The putts should be at least 15 feet in length.

Scoring is as follows: 3 points for a made putt (the equivalent of a ringer in Horseshoes), 1 point for the closest to the hole (again, like in Horseshoes).

If neither player makes a putt, but Player A's two putts wind up closer to the cup than either one of Player B's putts, Player A gets two points.

If neither makes a putt, but Player A has the closest ball and Player B the second closest ball, Player A gets one point.

In a popular variation of the basic game, if Player A makes a putt (3 points) and Player B puts one in on top of his, Player B gets 6 points and Player A's 3 points are taken off. (That's the equivalent of "covering a ringer with a ringer of your own" in horseshoes.)

The player who's scored on the previous two putts has the honor to go first on the next series. Play continues until one player reaches 21 points.

You know, just the mention of "Horseshoes" reminds me of the legendary Titanic Thompson, the golfer and hustler. He once beat the world champion horseshoes pitcher in a special exhibition match. Ti threw ringers all day, while the champ kept leaving his throws short of the mark.

Ti took the money he won in bets on the match and got out of town before the world champion found out that Ti had set up a 41-foot toss, *not* the regulation 40 feet. You'll read more about Titanic's hustles in later chapters.

Two Against One

Where one player has putting abilities clearly inferior to another player's, he may wish to even up any putting game by proposing My Two Against Your One, a game that is self-explanatory.

The superior putter should be cautious in playing this game, however. Even bad to poor putters will prove difficult to handle if you give them a second putt on a hole, because they will quickly see the correct line and the proper speed each putt requires.

Short and Not Hard Enough

Someone, probably the Yogi Berra of golf, once observed that 90 percent of the putts that are left short of the hole will not fall in.

Have you ever seen a putt dying short of the hole reaccelerate and roll into the cup? Of course not. But you probably have seen some putts go past the front of the cup and then fall in the side or swing around and sneak in the back door.

A putt that reaches the hole is a putt that at least has a chance to fall. One that's left short doesn't.

Thus we have the putting game Short and Not Hard Enough. It's a game that penalizes a player any time he leaves a putt short that would either tie or win the hole outright.

The players agree at the outset what the penalty will be on each putt left short. Then they remember to charge their putts. The game is that simple.

The name of the game, by the way, reminds me of a friend who tells me that his wife often complains that....oh, never mind.

Three Point Putts

This is another practice game designed to help you improve your putting skills. It rewards a player for reaching the hole or being past it.

You can play Three Point Putts with one or more opponents. All the competing players stroke one putt on each hole and only one player—whoever is closest to the hole—receives points.

The player closest to the hole receives a minimum of one point. He receives two points if he's closest to the hole and past the cup—three points for sinking a putt.

If several players sink putts on the same hole, they each receive three points. But again, if no one sinks a putt, only the player closest to the hole earns points.

The game is usually played for 9 or 18 holes on the practice green. It's a good game to play while you're waiting to be called to the first tee because you can stop after any hole.

A scoring variation of this game is to award no points for being short on a hole (even if it's closest), two points for being past, and three points for making the putt.

Putt By The Foot

This is a putting game that rewards the player who can make the ball disappear into the cup from long distances.

Close doesn't count in Putt By the Foot. Neither does consistency nor a smooth putting stroke. What counts is an ability to sink long putts.

It's a game that gives the player who's having a mediocre day with his irons something to stay excited about. Because if that player sinks several long putts, he can still make some serious money on the green.

The game typically is played for a fixed amount per foot on all putts made. A player who snakes in several 20- or 30-footers during a round can go home with a thick roll in his money clip, even if he shoots 100.

This is one of my favorite golf games. There's nothing like "steppin' 'em off" after ramming in a long putt. Especially since each step means money.

If you haven't tried this game with a group, I'd suggest you try it next time out. I guarantee you'll like it.

Nine Twos

This is a putting game designed to increase a player's ability to hit "lag" putts. Ben Smith, the Senior PGA Tour player, says the game is a popular one on East Texas courses.

As the name implies, the object of Nine Twos is to take two putts on all nine holes on the practice putting green. A player who makes a one or takes three putts loses to the player who scores a two.

Playing the game will help a golfer focus on the right speed for stroking putts and help him get consistent length on the lag putts.

Nine Twos is sometimes played in conjunction with Three-Point Putts, which rewards getting to the hole or past it.

I've discovered that although putting games like Nine Twos are most fun when several players are involved, they can also be played individually.

I'd recommend that players who are practicing by themselves use some goal-oriented game like Nine Twos rather than just hitting putts at random. This is a good practice game, one that's considerably more difficult than it may at first seem.

Eleven

In this putting game, players accumulate points toward a total of Eleven. To win the game, you must hit Eleven exactly. If you exceed the total, or bust, you have to start over.

Eleven can be played by several players at once. Points are awarded like this: five points for sinking a putt and one point for being the closest to the hole.

If a player with 8 points total sinks a putt he busts Eleven with 13 and his score reverts to 2.

It's simple to score and it's fun to play, regardless of the stakes.

Quarter

Quarter is a household putting game for bachelors or golfers with understanding wives. Real understanding.

Drill a hole into a Quarter, then nail or screw the coin into your carpet so that it creates a slight depression, like a golf cup. Use the Quarter as your indoor golf hole and play all the other putting games you'd normally play on the practice green, giving bonus points for putts that stop exactly on the quarter.

Speaking of playing on the carpet, I was out in Palm Springs for the Bob Hope Desert Classic in the early 1960s, staying with Bob and Basie McCulloch, the chainsaw and power tool people.

We were having cocktails one evening when Bob said, "Doug, I've been having trouble with my short irons. Would you show me what I'm doing wrong?" Bob's den had high ceilings, which permitted a full swing, and a thick shag carpet. I proceeded to give a demonstration on the intricacies of short-iron play.

On my third swing, a 10-inch cut of that expensive carpet went flying into the air and I nearly collapsed at the thought of having taken such an expensive divot. But after letting me apologize profusely and squirm with discomfort, the McCullochs let me in on the joke. It seems that Bob had taken that divot (accidentally, of course) about two weeks earlier. He just put it back in place and decided he had a trap baited for someone like me. I don't know who else he tricked, but I'm certain he got at least $5,000 worth of enjoyment at my expense that night.

Sawagi

This putting game takes its name from a Japanese word that means "excitement."

It can add a great deal of excitement to your round of golf, too.

Sawagi is a bet that applies on all players whose approach shots land outside the length of the pin, roughly eight feet.

If a player one-putts the green, he wins a unit from the other players.

If the player two-putts the green, it's a push with the others.

But if he three-putts, he owes the others a unit.

The Japanese are some of the most avid golfers and golf fans in the world, and Japan has some of the world's most beautiful courses.

Some of the most beautiful women, too.

Getting A Group Together

Who you play golf with is often more important than where or when you play, because it's likely to have a greater effect on how you play.

Some players bring out the best in others, and some players have the exact opposite effect. I remember several occasions in the 1960s when Arnold Palmer and Jack Nicklaus were paired together, that their own great rivalry seemed to have a negative effect on their games.

They got so wrapped up in beating each other that the importance of their individual matchup seemed to supersede the importance of tournament itself. On more than one occasion, The King and The Golden Bear started playing beyond their own enormous capabilities— like a baseball pitcher who starts overthrowing—and neither one of them had a good round.

I can truthfully say the rest of us liked to see those two golfing gods paired together because it gave us mortals a chance to win.

Their great friend and rival Gary Player used to play a lot of practice rounds with Arnie and Jack until he figured out it was harmful to his game. To try to stay within hailing distance of them off the tee, Player started swinging from the heels, which disrupted his rhythm and timing on the other shots.

He finally figured out it was better to play the Tuesday practice rounds with someone else and leave the driving to Palmer and Nicklaus.

Chemistry has a great deal to do with finding good golfing partners. The players in your group, assuming you're looking to set up a regular game, should have several things in common. In my opinion, the most critical factors are skill level, disposition, dedication, and betting temperament.

Let's look at each one:

SKILL. You can argue the point that handicaps can be used to put everyone on a par with everyone else, but I don't think several dots on the scorecard can compensate for physical and psychological gaps between good golfers and ones that are mediocre or worse.

I've always felt that the best games are those matching players of near-equal ability. A foursome of players with handicaps from 3 to 5 will make for a good match, as will a foursome with handicaps from 15 to 20. (The higher the players' handicaps, the more range is tolerated between average scores.)

But a foursome where two players are below 10 and two are above 20 seldom lends itself to a pleasurable outing. The high-handicappers often try to "do too much" to keep up with the better players and only in the process wind up damaging their already fragile games. The low-handicappers, meanwhile, usually have trouble with concentration and experiment too much for their own good.

A lot of tournament formats try to match up golfers with varying abilities (foursomes are comprised of A, B, C and D players), and I think that's fine for an occasional tournament. But I don't believe that mix of talent would work well in a regular game.

I think it's true that an average player benefits from playing with a good player and a good player benefits from playing with an excellent player. My advice is to try to compete with players who are at, or just slightly above, your own level. Occasionally you'll leave your group behind or they'll leave you behind, but it will take a while for the shift to occur.

DISPOSITION. Golfers, certainly amateur ones, run the gamut from Mr. Intensity, who plays each hole like it's the final one of a U.S. Open championship, to Mr. Laissez-Faire, who plays golf like it's a day at the beach and his game is a sand castle: magnificent one moment and washed up the next.

We've all known, and played with, golfers with varied dispositions on the course. Happy-go-lucky guys. Vocal guys and quiet guys. Guys who are upbeat or downbeat, demonstrative or subdued, calm or irate.

Since I'm the outgoing type, I prefer to play with other outgoing types like the Chi-Chi's and the Lee Trevino's. Not only do we enjoy the golf, but we try to make sure that the galleries are entertained. I've always considered myself more of an entertainer than an athlete, anyway.

My favorite playing partner of all time was Al Besselink. That was mainly because Bessie, like me, kept an eye out for the attractive ladies in our gallery. We were known to double date in the evening with women we'd met on the course during our round.

Bessie was the kind of guy who liked to carry a rose in his teeth during a round. Sometimes he'd take the rose and give it to a winsome lass he spied behind the ropes. Bessie had wavy blond hair and at 6'4" and 225 pounds he looked like a Greek God. In fact, that's what people called him, "The Greek God." When he missed a putt that cost us money, though, I changed his nickname to "The goddam Greek."

Bessie would have been an even better golfer had he not been such a good card player. His gin games usually kept him up until all hours of the night, and he sometimes ran out of steam on the golf course. But he was the best playing partner imaginable, always in a good mood, always with a twinkle in his eye and never afraid of the action.

Since my policy has always been to be nice to everyone, playing partners have never been a problem for me. I've gotten along well with the extroverts as well as the quiet ones like Art Wall, Gene Littler, Don January, and Julius Boros.

I especially enjoyed playing with guys like Sam Snead, Jimmy Demaret, and Tommy Bolt, guys who were heroes when I was still a youngster on the pro circuit. Playing with them was an education in itself. I also had the privilege of being paired with Ben Hogan several times near the end of his legendary career. That, obviously, was a major-league thrill.

I hope all my playing partners through the years enjoyed playing with me as much as I enjoyed playing with them.

Of course, in professional golf, the pairings are made for you, depending on your daily standing within a particular tournament. We don't get to tell the pairings committee who we'd like to play with on a given day.

In your regular golfing game, though, you can shape the squad. And my advice is to look for a blend of people who possess on the one hand a strong competitive spirit and a desire to play, and on the other hand a sense of humor and the ability to roll with the punches.

I'd caution you against having a regular game with a player who can't control his temper. The kind of guy who lets the golfing gods get under his skin and proceeds to make an ass out of himself by throwing clubs, screaming expletives, or wreaking havoc on the course.

Anger has a place in golf only when it can be channeled from a negative to a positive. Like in tennis, where the best thing a player can do after losing his service is to immediately break his opponent back, the best thing a golfer can do is follow a bogey or double-bogey with a birdie.

I can't tell you how many times I've seen a guy like Palmer follow a bogey with a birdie. He'd knock the cover off of his next tee shot, attack the flag on his approach iron and ram his birdie putt into the cup. Palmer knew best: Don't get mad, get even.

And that's the sign of a champion, regardless of the sport. The athlete who can keep his cool in the face of adversity. The person who can overcome one bad shot, by not making another one.

Besides an ill-tempered player, the other type to avoid at all costs is the self-absorbed. The kind of player who's so wrapped up in his own little world that he adds no spirit, to life, no *camaraderie* to the game.

You're out on the golf course to have fun—and win some money. It ain't a game of chess.

The most self-absorbed player, of course, was Ben Hogan. He believed he needed to block out every potential distraction—galleries, officials, even his playing partners—to play his best golf, so he did. His record speaks for itself, so he obviously knew what he was doing.

Hogan was a genius with a golf club, certainly one of the two or three best players ever, but I don't think you want his personality type in your regular game. Sam Snead once joked that he'd played an entire round with Hogan and the only words Ben had uttered all day were, "You're away, Sam."

But my favorite Hogan story concerns the year at the Masters he was paired with Claude Harmon. On the devilish par-3, 12th hole, Hogan whistled an iron toward the hole and the ball came to rest four feet from the cup. Then Harmon stepped to the tee and knocked his ball inside of Hogan—inside the cup, in fact, for a hole-in-one.

Hogan walked to the green without acknowledging Harmon's ace and sank his own birdie putt. Only then did Hogan acknowledge Harmon's feat. "Nice shot, Claude," was all he said.

The day you make an ace, I guarantee you'll want to be playing with the kind of group that will share in your jubilation.

DEDICATION. Everyone has his own set of priorities, and it's up to you to establish where golf fits in yours. It also makes sense that the other players in your game attach the same relative value to the game.

The serious player is precisely that, serious about his game. Regardless of skill level, he takes a dedicated approach. He'll be there come rain or come shine. The less serious player, who has a take-it-or-leave-it attitude won't work well in that environment.

Before locking in your game, make sure that each of the players has a shared sense of commitment. It will eliminate problems down the line, believe me.

BETTING TEMPERAMENT. Some guys have golf games where no money changes hands. Some play for small amounts. I've known millionaires, business tycoons, who play for fifty a side. Fifty cents, not fifty dollars.

I've also known guys who had the personal fortunes—and the love of action—that would play for several grand a hole. Every day.

Where you fit in the gambling spectrum, from high-rollers to the two-bitters, doesn't matter one whit. What matters is that the financial perimeters that are established are acceptable to all parties involved.

Trying to mix guys who want to play for big numbers and like plenty of side action with guys who like maybe a $2 Nassau tops is like putting a snake and mongoose together.

You're going to have a mess on your hands.

There's probably one other area in which your group should have some compatibility: habadashery habits. That's right, your attire.

Take it from a guy who knows about dressing for success on the golf course. If you look like a million bucks, you'll feel good about yourself and you'll probably play up to your potential.

You know the feeling you get when you put on your best business suit with a freshly starched dress shirt and an elegant tie? You'll have the same feeling of poise and presence when you put on a fine cardigan golf sweater or a highly-polished pair of lace-up golf shoes.

Whether you wear the conservative gray and white of a Ben Hogan or the proud-as-a-peacock color schemes of a Doug Sanders isn't important, either; but having golf attire that is fresh, clean and crisp will add to your own feeling of self-confidence.

I'd say it's worth a half a stroke a side.

Whether you prefer to play in threesomes, foursomes, sixsomes or even gangsomes should be of no particular concern. As you'll read in the following three sections, there are a variety of golf games for groups of all sizes.

What is important is that everyone be happy with the company he keeps.

So don't choose your groups in hully-gully fashion. Get a game that's a good match in several key areas and not only will you enjoy the experience more, but you'll likely play better as a result.

Gangsome Games

Oklahoma Whip-Out

Not a gambling game itself, Oklahoma Whip-Out refers to a system for settling debts among players. It's most commonly used in gangsome games, because of the number of side bets that need to be settled.

Oklahoma Whip-Out stipulates that all side bets must be settled in cash at the end of each hole. Only after all the money has changed hands can play begin on the next hole.

Golfers who grew up playing in Oklahoma, like TV and motion picture star James Garner, are accustomed to abiding by those terms.

Settling up after each hole eliminates the possibility that mistakes or disagreements will occur later on. It also keeps a lot of bills and coin changing hands, another psychological stimulant.

Finally, and many would say most important of all, you find out early if your opponents "forgot to bring cash" that day.

Horserace
(Also Known as Texas Shootout)

This popular special event is usually played before or after regular tournaments. It involves at least 10 individuals or 10 teams and is usually played as a nine-hole event.

Each player (or team) antes up the given amount, be it $10, $20, or $100. Play begins on the first (or tenth) hole and on each hole the person or team posting the highest score is eliminated.

Say on the first hole, two players (or teams) birdie, four players par, and four players bogey. The six players that made birdie or par automatically get to advance to the second hole, while the four bogey-shooters engage in a quick playoff (either putting or chipping) to see which one is eliminated on that hole.

On each successive hole, one player or team is eliminated. The winner ultimately is determined on the ninth green, if necessary by a playoff.

The Colonial NIT in Fort Worth, which I won in 1961, includes a Horserace in the week's activities. They call it a Texas Shootout, naturally. The players enjoy it and so do the fans, primarily because it's something out of the ordinary.

Beginning this year, in fact, I'm going to add a horserace to my Doug Sanders Kingwood Celebrity Classic in Houston. We all like to try something new from time to time, and golfers are no different. That's the reason for publishing this book of golf games. My goal is to help golfers of all abilities derive more pleasure and satisfaction from the game.

Cross Country

This is a popular game that can happen spontaneously or be more calculated. It involves imagination, creativity, an adventurous spirit, a love of nature and a sense of humor. Cross Country golf isn't for everyone, but those who've tried it never forget the experience.

Perhaps the best known Cross Country golf game was the one novelist Dan Jenkins played in his hometown of Fort Worth. Jenkins wrote about the game and the players, disguising names to protect the guilty parties, first in a Sports Illustrated article and later in his golfing novel *Dead Solid Perfect.*

The Cross Country game started at Worth Hills C.C. on the southwest edge of the TCU campus. Jenkins and cohorts—usually a dozen entrants entered the field, though how many finished is another matter—would play down past TCU's fraternity and sorority row, in front of Amon Carter Stadium, where greats like Sammy Baugh and Davey O'Brien once played, through the stadium parking lot, along

the hilly, winding roads of the development known as Colonial Hills, in front of the entrance to the famous Colonial Country Club, over the security fence and finish on the first green at Colonial. The hole stretched roughly 3.5 miles.

Jenkins and his pals would putt out and then run like hell before the Colonial security force could catch them.

Another scene of Cross Country games was Tenison Park in Dallas, where Lee Trevino learned to hustle. One of the famous games at Tenison was the "Tunnel Hole." A gangsome of players would start at the 10th tee on the west course, play through a tunnel cut through a railroad trestle, hit down the 17th fairway of the east course (Tenison has two 18-hole layouts) through another tunnel and back up the first fairway on the east course to the 18th green. The Tunnel Hole stretched roughly 1,400 yards and played to a par 16. Legend has it that Titanic Thompson set the record by negotiating the hole in 9 strokes.

Cross Country is typically played within the confines of an 18-hole course. Players can design the game to whatever specifications they wish, and seldom is the same course selected more than once. Cross Country, obviously, is a game to be played at off-peak periods when traffic on the course permits.

Tee Markers

Darrell Royal, the former University of Texas football coach, likes to play Tee Markers, a game similar to Cross Country.

Coach Royal and his friends like to play as many holes as possible before rain or darkness stops them. Once they are interrupted, they head back to the clubhouse, but they play Tee Markers as they go.

If they've completed 22 holes in a round (a complete 18 and four extra holes), they'll throw balls down beside the 4th green and play back to the #4 tee. They "hole out" by hitting one of the tee markers. Then they play back down the 3rd, 2nd and 1st holes, finishing up on the 1st tee. Without fooling around with putting, they've found you can play 3 or 4 holes very quickly.

Three-In-One

Three-In-One is a great game for six players. It takes its name from the fact that within a group of six, three games of Best Ball can be played at once.

Teams are chosen with three players on each team. The match is played for Best Ball, Best Two Balls and Best Three Balls.

This is an excellent game, because one team may be winning the Best Ball portion but losing the other two bets. If you ever wind up with a group of six players, try Three-In-One.

Foursome Games

Bridge

Since Bridge is a popular game at country clubs, and many golfers have played a rubber or two in their time, it seems fitting to report that there's a golf game with the same name.

And just like the card game that inspired it, the golf game called Bridge involves a foursome and revolves around a bidding system. You can win bids, as well as doubled and redoubled bids. But you can't win a Grand Slam. That was reserved for Bobby Jones in 1930. Nor can you win a minor slam. That was reserved for Ben Hogan in 1953.

Here's how the golf game called Bridge works: It is usually played without handicaps between four players (two-man teams) of near equal ability. The scores of all four players are used on each hole. Each team initiates the bidding on alternate holes.

Team One will "bid" by projecting a combined score on the hole. Bidding cannot begin more than 3 strokes over par. So if the first hole is a par-4, or par-8 for two players, Team One's opening bid must be 11 or less.

Let's say Team One bids 10. The rules of Bridge stipulate that bids can only be made in increments of one or two, so Team Two has the following options:

It can bid either 9 or 8.

It can pass and let Team One play the hole for 10.

It can "double" the opening bid, which is another way of saying it doesn't think Team One can play the hole in 10 or less.

If Team Two doubles the bid, Team One can elect to redouble, just like in the card game. Or it can pass.

The hole is played out after the bidding ends. Team One can get two points for making its bid of 10 and one point for each stroke under the bid. If Team One fails to make 10, it loses two points plus one point for each stroke over 10. After these points are calculated, doubles and redoubles are figured.

On the second hole, Team Two takes control of the bidding. After that, the bids alternate for the remainder of the round.

Some action-oriented players find the standard scoring for Bridge too tame. To raise the stakes, they use the actual score as the betting unit. For example, if a team bids 10 on a hole and makes it, it wins 10 bets. It wins 20 bets if doubled and 40 if redoubled. An overtrick, which in golf would mean shooting 9 on a bid of 10, makes an extra bet won. The team in the example above would win 11, 22 or 44 bets.

Another wrinkle to Bridge is the in-flight double. This variation permits the team without the bid to double after either player on the bidding team has struck the ball (the double must be called before the ball lands, however). The double is used when it's immediately apparent that a shot is headed out of bounds or into a hazard.

To even things up, however, the hole is then scored as a "One-way" Redouble. Here's how it works:

Team A bids 10 and Team B passes. The best player on Team A hits a ball that appears to be headed out of bounds. Either player on Team B can shout "double." There is no provision to refuse (see the game *Hammer*) so the bet is now doubled. If Team A fails to shoot 10 on the hole, regardless of whether they shoot 11 or 15, Team B gets 20. But if Team A somehow manages to make 10 despite the O.B., the hole is scored as if it were redoubled, so Team A wins 40.

Bridge is primarily a foursome game, but it can also be played by two players, just like the card game Honeymoon Bridge. The bidding and rules for two golfers are exactly the same as for a foursome.

Personally, I've played Bridge on the golf course and Bridge at the card table, and while I like both games I still prefer gin rummy.

Wolf

Wolf is one of the most popular games foursomes play. It combines shotmaking and strategy, the elements of any good action.

The game works like this: On the first tee an order is established for the players, one through four. In some games, the sequence is set up by tossing balls, in others by the length of the drives on the first hole.

Player one is designated the Wolf for the first hole and has the option of choosing a partner for that hole. He normally selects the player with the best drive as his partner. The hole is then played as a low ball game with other bets like sandies and greenies in effect.

Player two becomes The Wolf on the second hole, and new teams are formed after tee shots are hit. Player three becomes the Wolf on the third hole, player four on the fourth hole, and on the fifth tee the Wolf reverts to player one and the rotation continues.

After 16 holes each player will have been the Wolf four times. Arrangements for holes 17 and 18 should be made on the first tee. In most games, the rotation will continue, but in some games the player who hits the long drive becomes the Wolf on 17 and 18.

One important note: Let's say the Wolf hits a good tee shot and the other three players muff their shots. The Wolf can choose to play the field, taking on the others by himself. If he loses to one player, he loses to all the others. If one player ties the Wolf, all tie. Obviously, if the Wolf wins the hole outright, he wins from everybody.

Some groups like to play a variation called Auto-Wolf, where every other time a player leads off he automatically takes on the field. This concept has merit, since some players would never play the field otherwise and because it gives good experience in dealing with pressure situations.

A variation of this game that's popular in the South and Southwest is to force the Wolf to make a decision on his partner after each tee ball. Say player two in the rotation hits a fairly good drive. The Wolf must say "Pass" or "Partner" immediately after that shot. If the Wolf passes on player two and players three and four chili-dip their shots, the Wolf can't go back and choose player two. The rule of thumb is to take anything half decent; the effect of the "No Return Rule" is to lessen somewhat the likelihood the players with the two best drives will be partners on the hole. It takes some of the bite out of the Wolf.

Another modification on par-3s definitely improves the game. The picker must go for Wolf, if he desires, *immediately* after hitting his shot but *before* any of the others hit. This adds more suspense to the greenie and team situations.

In any case, always check the scorecard to see who gets strokes, because handicaps make a big difference in this game.

Wolf is a good game for gangsomes to play, because there is always a way to even out the odds. Dick Martin and his pals at the Great Southwest Golf Club in Arlington, Texas, play the game with sixsomes. The Wolf and his partner must take as third partner the player with the worst drive on the whole.

The whole nature of Wolf is knowing the strengths and weaknesses of your playing partners. Keep a "book" on them and decide the types of situations and types of holes when you'd want them on your side.

The aspect of picking a partner can be subtle. Many times the player with the best tee ball will blow up on a hole. Often you'll find the best short game players aren't the best off the tee. And keep in mind the golfing axiom: It's not how you drive, it's how you arrive.

To my knowledge the all-time worst pick at Wolf was made by Tom Marz at Hearthstone C.C. in Houston several years ago. It was on a par-3 hole, so he had to choose his ball immediately or select another one. As it happened, the pin was on the back of the green, behind a small hump. Marz thought he hit long on the hole, so he passed on his shot. He chose another player's shot that he could see. When the group reached the green, they discovered Tom's ball in the cup. He had passed up an ace!

One other variation of this game is called Wolf and Pig. Here, if you get selected as the Wolf's partner, you have the opportunity to "Pig It," that is to play the others in the field yourself.

All bets are doubled, and the Wolf winds up playing the hole with the players he originally passed on.

Vegas

(Also called Daytona)

Vegas is a popular game with foursomes. It keeps all members of the group involved since the combined scores of each two-person team are used on each hole. It is an expensive version of low ball/low total.

Here's how Vegas works: On the par four 1st hole, Team A players shoot 4 and 5. Team B players shoot 4 and 6. Team A wins, 45 to 46, and goes up one unit.

On the second hole, another par four, Team A posts a 5 and 7, while Team B posts another 4 and 6. This time, Team B wins by eleven units—difference between 46 and 57. After two holes, Team B leads Team A by 10 units.

Where Vegas gets expensive is when one team scores a birdie. In those cases, the score of the team that loses the hole is reversed. Had the second hole in the example above been a par five, Team B's birdie 4 would have meant that Team A's 57 would be reversed to 75. The difference between 46 and 75 is 29 units—a significant difference on one hole.

If a player shoots 10 or more, his team's score gets reversed even if his partner wins low ball. If one team has a 3 and a 10 and the other 4 and 6, the scores are 103 to 46. That's a way to lose a hole and still win money.

Bisques

My old friend Charles Price, the noted golf writer who recently won the Golf Writers Association of America's Gold Journalism Award, reminded me of this game, which was popular in the 1920s and '30s.

Bisques are strokes that you can take whenever you want. Let's say for example, that two players are 6- and 11-handicappers. Instead of the 11-handicapper getting five shots where they fall on the card, he is given two (or possibly three) Bisques.

A player can take a bisque after the hole is played, but only one per hole can be used. These are more powerful than mere handicap strokes, because they can be used at the player's discretion.

Bisques are extremely valuable in games where carryovers are being played.

Ten Cents A Hole

John Oram and the members of his foursome at Sleepy Hollow Country Club in Scarborough, New York, have been known to play low ball for ten cents a hole.

High-rollers, huh?

But you should also know that the bet doubles on every hole and they play carryovers. By the back nine, the wager has really started to mount.

Here's what the payoff in the game looks like.

HOLE	PAYOFF	HOLE	PAYOFF
1	$.10	10	51.20
2	.20	11	102.40
3	.40	12	204.80
4	.80	13	409.60
5	1.60	14	819.20
6	3.20	15	1,638.40
7	6.40	16	3,276.80
8	12.80	17	6,553.60
9	25.60	18	$13,107.20

All I can suggest is that the next time someone tells you on the first tee that he wants to play for a dime a hole, make sure you get a clarification on the terms.

This sounds like an exciting game to me, but for most golfers this game would be far beyond their comfort level. I'd also bet that anyone who plays this game spends extra time practicing on the closing holes.

I sure as hell would.

Threesome Games

Nine

You've been a member of a regular weekend foursome for years. But one Saturday a member of the group becomes a no-show.

So what do you do? Go home and catch up on the "Honey Do" chores? Put in some extra hours at the office? Or do you take a flier on a new fourth and let your money ride in the hands of a stranger?

Maybe you choose none of the above. Instead, you adjust for the absence of a member of your group by playing a game for threesomes. One of the best you'll find is a game called Nine. Here's how to play Nine: Each hole carries a value of 9 points. You agree on a standard unit per point—whatever is in your comfort zone. That may be fifty cents or fifty bucks.

The winner of a hole gets 5 points, the runnerup gets 3 points and the loser gets 1 point. If the players shoot 4, 5, 6 the scoring is simple.

CHAPTER THIRTEEN

But if one player shoots 5 and the other two players shoot 6, the point breakdown is 5-2-2. If two players tie with 5 and the third player shoots a 6, the point breakdown is 4-4-1. If all three players tie on the hole, the point breakdown is 3-3-3.

At the end of the round, you add up each player's points, multiply by the unit bet and see each player's winnings. The losers make up the difference between their total and the winner's.

Regular Nine players tell me that the scoring tends to even out over 18 holes. Nine is a fun, competitive game in which every shot means something on nearly every hole. After all, tying for second sure beats being last all alone.

Captain

When only three members of a foursome show up, golfers can play a game called Captain that's patterned after three-man gin rummy.

A Captain is selected for the round, and that person begins the match playing one of the two opponents. If the Captain wins the first hole, he changes opponents. If the Captain loses or ties the first hole, he keeps the same opponent on the next hole, and until he wins a hole.

Although you may wonder if one of the two opponents might be out of action too much, it's common for players to cook up enough side action to keep everyone's interest throughout the round. As in the game of gin rummy, the Captain is paid double when he wins. He also pays double when he loses, however.

Whenever someone looks at me and says, "Gin?" I answer, "You bet—golf, cards or a drink?"

Par for A Partner

Depending on the skill level of the players involved, threesomes sometimes allow one player to have an imaginary partner who shoots net pars on every hole. That player (and Par) take on the other two players in a Best Ball game using handicaps.

For high-handicappers, the game might be better structured by giving the one player net Bogey For A Partner.

I suppose you could adjust this game to even higher levels, but I'm not going to recommend it. If I had to take Double-Bogey For A Partner on every hole, I'd start drinking *seriously*.

Worst of Two Players

This threesome game is similar to Captain, in that one player takes on the other two. Except Player A is competing against the worst score of Players B and C.

If on the first hole Player A shoots 4, Player B shoots 4 and Player C shoots 5, then Player A wins the hole 4–5.

If the scores on the hole are A-4, B-3, and C-5, Player A still wins the hole 4–5.

Old-timer J.T. Yates likes to tell about the time he was playing this game against Spiz Berg and Howie Johnson at Memorial Park in Houston in the early 1950s. Spiz was the city champion that year, and Howie Johnson went on to become a PGA player and now is a regular on the Senior PGA Tour.

As good as Berg and Johnson were, they couldn't beat J.T. Yates at this one. In fact, Worst of Two got the best of Berg and Johnson. They quit after 9 holes, not only because they were losing money but they were straining their friendship as well.

I can see where this game would be tough on any twosome, since someone "let the other guy down" on nearly every hole.

Do the Hustle

In the game of golf, just like in the game of life, some people are always trying to put things over on others.

There's a breed of golf gambler who spends a high percentage of his waking hours planning ways to separate other golfers from their money. These gamblers prefer to be paid in cash—but they also accept major credit cards, personal checks, bearer bonds and all other negotiable instruments.

These people deal in bets (propositions) that they make to anyone unwitting enough to accept them (suckers). They have absolutely no qualms about misrepresenting their true abilities to slant the terms of the game in their favor. When they have everything set up to their satisfaction, they call the game a "free-roll" or "the nuts."

These people are known as hustlers.

The most famous golf hustler ever was Alvin Clarence Thomas, better known as Titanic Thompson. His life as a gambler was the stuff of legends. In fact, Damon Runyon used Titanic as the inspiration for the character Sky Masterson in his Broadway hit "Guys and Dolls."

Titanic, or Ti as everyone called him, was an expert card player, card thrower, coin tosser, con man and hustler. He took up the game of golf as a diversion from the marathon card games he was playing in San Francisco with his partner Nick (The Greek) Dandolos.

Ti was a natural at golf. Legend has it the first time he swung a driver, he hit the ball more than 300 yards. He knew at once that golf presented another avenue for getting into suckers' wallets.

In his first golf hustle, as told in Carlton Stowers' biography, *The Unsinkable Titanic Thompson,* Ti lost all nine holes of a $10-a-hole match to a San Francisco pro. Thompson hit the ball all over the course and grumbled about how tough the game was. That same evening, Ti proposed that if the pro would give him one stroke a hole the next day Ti would be willing to play for $1,000 a hole.

The pro, a fellow named Brainer, accepted. Thompson found no small amount of side action eager to be bet against him. The next morning, though, Ti removed the camouflage from his true ability. He didn't lose a single hole during the match, making it a no-Brainer. Thompson walked away with more than $50,000 in his pocket and a new hustle in his repertoire.

Titanic got his nickname at a pool hall in Joplin, Missouri, in 1912, the same year the luxury ocean liner sank on its maiden voyage. He'd been running rack after rack and cleaning out all comers when a latecomer to the game asked a local gambler named Snow Clark who the hotshot was. Clark allowed as how he didn't know, but the guy should be called Titanic 'cause he was sinking everybody in the parlor.

Thompson's pet golf hustle was to hack out a few rounds in the 100s playing righthanded, all the while setting up some well-heeled suckers. Then he'd bait them by claiming they had no talent at the game and suggesting they give it up.

"Why I could beat your sorry asses playing left-handed," Thompson would say, watching as first the suckers' blood pressure, and then the amount they were willing to wager, would rise.

Ti was left-handed, of course.

Like most golf hustlers, Thompson could play a legitimately good game. He once shot a 29 on the back nine at Ridglea C.C. in Fort

Worth to beat the great Byron Nelson in a head-up match. Ti took some serious money off of Lord Byron's backers that afternoon.

Later, as his golfing abilities declined, Ti used his considerable powers of persuasion to set up other games of chance—actually, they were games of no-chance if you bet against him.

For example, Ti liked to stand on the practice green at Tenison Park in Dallas, a haven for golf hustlers, and pitch silver dollars at one of the cups from 20 away or more. He'd land the coins all around the cup, but somehow none ever went in.

Presently, a crowd would gather to watch and Ti would start baiting the hook. "I reckon I could make one out of three tosses for $100," he'd say. Everyone in the crowd would remain silent, watching Thompson miss toss after toss.

"I reckon I could make two out of three," he'd say. The on-lookers kept quiet.

"I reckon if I really had to I could make three out of three," Ti would finally say. At which point someone invariably stepped forward and took the bet.

And in a flash, the three silver dollars would arc swiftly out of Ti's hands and fall into the cup.

Rat-tat-tat.

Ti's hustles could be spontaneous as well. He once bet a friend $100 that he could induce the friend's prized bird dog, which had been tagging along during their round of golf, to start barking within 60 seconds.

Ti's friend, having trained the dog himself, took the bet. He knew his dog as well as he knew his own wife—maybe better, in fact. He knew the dog wouldn't bark just to hear itself bark.

But what he didn't know was that the eagle-eyed Thompson had seen a jackrabbit hiding in a depression near the edge of the fairway, roughly 100 yards away.

Ti set up for his drive and promptly hit a low screamer that strafed the ground near the jackrabbit. The rabbit took off across the fairway and as soon as it did the bird dog gave chase.

Barking loudly, of course.

Ti's hustle reminds me of the one about Mike Windham and the pigeons. Mike plays out of Royal Oaks C.C. in Dallas, where a large flock of pigeons has been known to congregate.

The pigeons were huddled one afternoon in the middle of the fairway, probably 260 yards from the tee. Windham's playing partner spotted the pigeons and said to him, "Bet you $50 I can make them fly."

Although his playing partner was a long-hitter, Windham accepted the proposition. It seemed like a wise decision, too, when the bettor snap-hooked his drive no more than 200 yards off the tee.

At the same time, though, the bettor started yelling at the top of his lungs and, to Windham's everlasting astonishment, the pigeons all flew away.

Windham, who wins his share of side action, probably felt like a pigeon himself when he paid off his playing partner, who happened to be my friend Gary Boren.

About the only hustlers' game at which Titanic Thompson didn't excel was called Lakewood Golf. A bunch of Thompson's cronies in Dallas played a game at Lakewood C.C. that permitted players to create any distraction or diversion to rattle their opponents.

The only rules were you couldn't touch the player or his ball as he was playing to hit. Otherwise, anything was legal. Anything, including blowing up balloons and letting the air out (you know what *that* sounds like) just as a player was about to putt. Or firing blanks from a .38 revolver in the middle of a player's backswing.

A favorite ploy the guys used when Ti was addressing the ball was to drive a golf cart straight at him, swerving at the last instant to avoid contact. Ti's pals would take the manifold off a gas-powered cart, and it made as much noise as a jet airplane taking off. Even the unsinkable Titanic sank under that pressure.

Titanic Thompson passed away in Fort Worth in the mid-1970s, but his legend lives on. It's safe to say that as long as golfers gather in the 19th hole to swap stories and lies, they'll tell tales of Titanic Thompson.

Tall ones.

Another of the best golf hustlers I've ever known is a fellow named Dick Martin. Dick's in his 70s now, and keeps a lower profile, but

back in his heyday there wasn't a golf gambler alive who hadn't heard of "Dandy Dick Martin of Dallas."

Martin hustled golf games all over the Southwest, winning golf tournaments—and the calcuttas that accompanied them—in six separate decades dating back to the 1930s. When Dick visited my home in Houston last fall, he told me that he still has possession of the first trophy he ever won. It was for a tournament held in Dallas in 1931. Between then and now, Dick may have won more golf tournaments than any human being who ever lived.

I'm not talking about The Masters or the U.S. Open, but more on the order of local and regional events. And always in the championship flight, I guarantee you.

It's not far-fetched to say Dick Martin could have been a household name as a golf professional. Lee Trevino wrote in his biography *They Call Me Super Mex*, ". . . [And] there was Dick Martin, probably the best player I ever saw until Jack Nicklaus."

It's just that Dick Martin was too busy hustling and gambling at golf to bother with being a PGA player.

His motto is "I won't play for fun . . . and I won't skip one." That's his way of saying he wants something riding on every hole he plays. On occasion, his thirst for action would force him to make propositions not entirely favorable to himself. ("When there ain't no suckers in the room, you're it," he likes to say.)

Of course that didn't happen much.

Dick Martin had the presence of mind to realize that in the wide world of golf, there are 100 high-handicappers for every scratch player like himself. And in those 100 high-handicappers are bound to be some with disposable income—dollars ready to be thrown away to Dandy Dick.

Martin was a master of creating games like "Pitch" and "Chip Again" which were designed to *balance* the game between himself and his opponents. Somehow, the scales never swung back to the center: they always tilted slightly to Martin's side.

I know a bit about *balancing* myself. After my college days at the University of Florida, I started hanging out at the LaGorce course near Miami Beach. It was an action-oriented club where you could play any game you could name for any amount you could count.

At that time, I probably played to a minus 5 handicap, meaning I averaged 67 a round. I had standing games with a bunch of monied players who carried 10s and 11 handicaps from the members' tees.

When I played them, I'd insist that the game was from the championship tees, which added four strokes to their game. Nor did I mention my minus 5, claiming only to be a "scratch" player.

Basically, I played for a year giving guys 10 or 11 shots when I had a real margin of 19 strokes.

All I had to do to win those games was stay conscious. Guys around the club were always asking me why I didn't turn pro, and I thought to myself, "Not when I have this golden goose . . ."

Two old-time PGA stars, Dutch Harrison and Herman Keiser, had a doozy of a two-man hustle that they worked successfully for years.

Dutch was one of the best at making the proposition. He liked to move in on a posh country club and challenge the club champion and runner-up to a foursome match. Dutch would propose some high stakes and take as much side action as he could get.

On the morning of the match, Dutch would show up at the first tee and claim that his partner was sick and couldn't play. He'd talk like the match was off, but then he'd reconsider.

"What the hell," Dutch would boast, "I could probably beat the two of you with a caddie as my partner."

That statement always led to new bets being taken against the pro. Dutch then would go down to the caddyshack to survey the crop and pick a partner.

His partner, naturally, would turn out to be Keiser, a solid enough player himself to have won the 1946 Masters over Ben Hogan.

Harrison and Keiser would clean up on the action and leave the club's members talking about the "best goddam caddie you've ever seen."

One noteworthy thing about golf hustlers is they'll bet on just about anything. One well-known hustler once called out a $500 bet to his playing partners that he had the smallest male member of all those assembled.

No sooner had he made the proposition than one of the high-rollers in the group dropped his trousers and revealed an organ of child-like proportion.

"Dead-heat," exclaimed the hustler, keeping his fly zipped up. "No action."

Another noteworthy thing about golf hustlers is that their golden rule goes like this: *Do unto others as they would do unto you, only do it to them first.*

For example, a fast golf cart can easily be worth 1.5 strokes a side to a hustler. It's uncanny how many clean lies he'll get in the fairway and playable lies in the rough.

I knew a hustler who on the way to his own ball was prone to mete out punishment to his playing partner's ball. On one occasion, he tossed his partner's ball into a water hazard, only to discover after closer inspection that it was his own ball he'd sunk.

Golf hustlers are well known for improvising shots. A Dallas hustler named Mose Brooks, a fine player in his own right, had occasional streaks of wildness with his driver. Now and then he'd wind up in the woods, facing disaster.

Mose had a perfect solution for those tight situations. He'd turn to his caddy and say, "Here, little pro, see if you can get us out."

Brooks' caddy was young Lee Elder, the best black golfer of all time. Lee would bail Brooks out and Mose would go on his merry way.

Not all golf pros have an affinity for golf gambling, however. Some pros I know play the game for its own sake, oblivious to some of the action around them.

A hustler I know once took Ben Smith, now one of the regulars on the PGA Senior Tour, down to Granbury, Texas, where he'd set up a game with the local pro. The hustler planned to pass Ben off as a scratch player, when he's obviously several strokes better than that.

Ben, who wasn't in on the set-up, stood around in the pro shop, reading the literature on the wall. He noticed something on the wall about an upcoming charitable event for PGA members.

When the pro came in, introductions were made all around. Then Ben asked him harmlessly, "Have you entered this tournament?"

When the pro answered affirmatively, Ben said he planned to send in his own entry as soon as he got back home.

No sooner were the words out of Ben's mouth than the hustler grabbed him by the arm and marched him toward the door. "That's it, Ben," he said. "We're going back to Dallas."

The proposition had been blown.

With all the golf gambling that went on at Tenison Park in Dallas during the heyday of Ti Thompson and the others, it was no surprise that on occasion the hustlers would be hijacked.

After all, these men would be carrying thousands of dollars on their persons, and what were they going to defend themselves with? Their ball-retrievers?

My favorite story, which several sources swear is true, concerns the time two masked gunmen jumped out of the bushes at Tenison and stopped a gangsome of high-stakes players.

They made the players stand in a line and used leg irons to shackle them together. The hijackers relieved the hustlers of their expensive wristwatches and other jewelry and their money clips. Their bulging money clips.

But before they did, one of the victims showed the quick wits that made him such a formidable hustler.

"Don't I owe you $500?" he asked the man on his right as he pulled his bankroll out of his pocket.

"That's right," said his friend, arms raised upward.

"Well here it is . . . now we're even," said the first fellow.

The hijackers got that, too.

Hustlers' Games

Chip Again

Dick Martin once arranged a game at Tenison Park in Dallas with a high-handicapper who was learning the game. To even things out, Dick agreed that his opponent, a fellow named Dennis Pierce, could knock Dick's ball off the green on every hole.

Using his putter, Pierce could knock Martin's ball in the bunker, in the rough or back down the fairway. He wasn't allowed, however, to hit Martin's ball into a water hazard. Then Martin had to chip on again and finish the hole.

After a long day of scrambling, Martin won the match, but just barely. He confessed he hadn't realized just how large a handicap he was allowing—there is a huge premium on being on the green in regulation, triggering the knock back.

This is one game (see Pitch for another) that helps even out play between a high-handicapper and low-handicapper. Next time you find yourself playing with someone who's 10–15 strokes better than you, suggest this game. Whether or not you win, it's a lot of fun to knock an opponent's ball away.

Paper Cup

Be careful if you're waiting for a game and a player comes up and says he'll play you hitting his shots from tee to green from inside a paper cup: You're about to be hustled.

What the hustler will do is place his ball inside a Dixie Cup for his drive and approach shots. What you may not know is that the plastic of the cup takes the spin off the shot. He'll hit it nearly as far as he normally would but without a hook or slice.

The only one who'll be in trouble is you, if you take his bet.

This reminds me of another old hustlers' trick—putting Vaseline on the face of a driver. It creates the same effect and gives the hustler a big edge over the unsuspecting. I'd say Mose Brooks was the best I ever saw at hitting out of a Dixie cup. Personally, I prefer to use paper cups for sipping my favorite beverages during strategy sessions in the 19th hole.

Putting for Birdie

Dick Martin was always looking to hustle up games with high-handicappers, on the educated premise that they had just as much money as low-handicappers and they were far more abundant.

One hustle Martin created was to allow his opponent to putt for birdie on every hole. The opponent would be on the par-3s in one, the par-4s in two and the par-5s in three. The caveat: Martin was allowed to place the ball where he wanted on the putting surface. He would leave his opponent a long, tricky putt on every hole.

Meanwhile, Martin would play the hole from the back tees.

What the high-handicapper soon learned was that his "advantage" wasn't enough to beat Martin, who consistently broke par. Martin was nearly always on the green in regulation and usually much closer to the hole than his opponent. Not only did Martin have easier putts, but he always got a "read" on the speed and slope of the green by watching his opponent putt first.

It's reasonable to assume that Martin saved this hustle to use at golf courses with large, undulating greens and not too much trouble from tee to green.

Otherwise Dick would have been hustling himself, and I promise you that rarely happened, if ever.

Foreplay

This suggestive name is given to a game where all shots must be executed with a four-iron. The four-iron is a good club to use, since it can be hit reasonable distances and also is an excellent club for chipping and putting.

Variations of the game are, of course, Fiveplay, Sixplay, Sevenplay and so on, but these games don't sound like nearly as much fun as Foreplay, do they?

Lee Trevino says that anyone who thinks he can beat the Merry Mex in a one-club match should apologize to him.

Playing with a single stick is the way many of us in the caddy ranks learned to play. Dutch Harrison, the Arkansas Traveler, was a master at opening or closing the face of the club and modifying his swing to produce dramatically longer or shorter shots. Guys like Harrison and Trevino could get as much as a five-club variance out of one stick.

Another big advantage in knowing how to get more or less distance from a given club is that you can drive your opponent to distraction. It will cure them from "playing out of your bag."

Tees Everywhere

In the game of Tees Everywhere, players can tee up any shot they wish. Fairway woods? Sure. Bunker shots? Why not?

The official rules of golf may frown on Tees Everywhere, but high-handicappers and latecomers to the game are all smiles once they've tried it. It certainly speeds up play of slow groups.

There used to be a bunch of golf hustlers in Dallas—guys like Red Whitehead, Dub Tyler, Joe Campisi, John Clark—who played a Tees Everywhere game at the old Village Country Club.

One day at the 8th hole, Jack Keller hit a tee shot on the 8th hole that went into a lake. The group was elated, since they didn't get into his money clip very often. But as it turned out the lake was only two feet deep and Keller could see his ball in the water. He reached into his bag and pulled out a 3-foot long tee. Keller waded into the lake, stuck his tee in the mud and hit his second shot on the green, saving the hole.

I love this story because the ultimate fun in winning is to beat a peer. A good gin player would rather beat another good player than a bad one, and the same holds true for a good golfer. And a hustler? There's *nothing* more amusing to me than to see one golf hustler trying to out-hustle another one.

Lakewood Golf

As I mentioned in the introduction to hustlers' games, a bunch of hustlers in Dallas used to play a game called Lakewood Golf. You could do anything you wanted to distract your opponent except physically interfere with him or his ball. Short of that, however, anything was permissible.

Talking, yelling, singing, popping balloons, firing off blanks—it all happened. One thing that proved to be extremely disconcerting was to have the flagstick swished over your head while you were trying to putt.

One time Jack Keller faced a slick downhill putt from about 10 feet, and just as he began his backstroke, one of the guys threw a pocketful of change at his feet. Jack yipped his putt so badly it rolled 20 feet past the hole, off the green and into a lake.

Red Whitehead says that of all the games he's played, and he's played a bunch, Lakewood Golf is far and away the funniest.

Pitch

This is a hustler's game for when the high-handicapper wants to hustle the low-handicapper. It can also be a way to even out the game when there's a wide variance in the abilities of playing partners.

The high-handicapper is given one free underhanded pitch on every hole. He can pitch his ball from out of bounds back into play. He can pitch his ball out of the woods or out of a trap. He can save himself a lot of strokes, in other words.

(Note: When I say "pitch" I mean a gentlemanly toss, not an overhanded peg à la Dale Murphy or Daryl Strawberry.)

A variation of Pitch is called "Drop." In Drop, the high-handicapper is entitled to a one arm's-length drop on every shot. That means he can improve his lie in the fairway, the rough or in a trap. It also means that on short putts, he may be able to drop the ball into the cup, saving a stroke. To keep it fun, though, the player's arm must be extended straight out on every drop.

Another variation is called "One Club Length, Anytime, Anywhere." In this game, you can improve your position one club length on every shot except on the green. As in Pitch, you sometimes can avoid an O.B. or get out of a hazard the easy way.

Murphies

A common thread running through many hustlers' games is a gimmick that seemingly "equalizes" players of widely different skills.

The operative word in the previous sentence is *seemingly*.

One such gimmick is a "Murphy."

A Murphy, more or less, is an option to have your opponent hit a shot over.

Let's say a scratch player and a 10-handicapper agree to a match. The scratch player might allow the 10-handicapper six Murphies as the handicap adjustment.

That would mean that on six separate occasions during the round the 10-handicapper could demand that the scratch player hit a shot over. He'd want to use his Murphies when the scratch player sank a long putt (a feat difficult to repeat) or when he hit an approach shot stiff to the flag.

The Murphies will save the 10-handicapper some shots, all right, but the better player still benefits disproportionately in this game. He'll be able to duplicate some good shots on his way into the higher-handicapper's hip pocket.

Just as in Chip, Pitch and other hustlers' games, the key critical factor is knowing the value of a given number of Murphies. The hustler knows the value and the neophyte doesn't. Guess who's going to win the bet?

Forgetting the hustlers for a moment, Murphies are fun for average golfers to try. Play your partners using regular handicaps and give each other an agreed-upon number of Murphies. Three or four Murphies are a good number, any more and the game deteriorates.

Murphies can't be used on crowded courses because they slow down play. But where conditions permit a more leisurely game, give Murphies a try. This game is really fun.

Worst of Two Shots

One of the most common hustlers' games begins with this statement: "I'll let you hit two balls on every shot, but you've got to play the worst of the two."

It's a bet you don't want to call unless you're an exceptional player. Otherwise, you're in for a long day.

Most professional players rank this among the toughest of all golf games. It's almost impossible to break 75—no matter how good you are.

I remember one time I bet an amateur who was nearly a scratch player that he couldn't break 100 in a round where he hit two balls on each shot and I got to call which shot he had to play next.

He came to the 18th tee needing a par. He hit two good drives, so it didn't matter which one I chose. Then he hit one iron shot to the green and one into a trap. Guess which one I made him play?

From the trap he hit one shot to 15 feet, but the other went past the pin by 30 feet. Guess which one I made him putt for par? He missed both 30-footers, took a five for 100 even, and I won the $100 bet.

Frankly, any format where more than one ball is hit and the worst of the shots is played makes an already difficult game damn near impossible.

Your Drive

Have you ever seen a golfer with a great short game hustle a big hitter? It happens all the time.

The accurate shotmaker will make the bet by saying "I'll use your drive and play you even." The big hitter—who usually has a big ego to match—will generally take the action.

He'll likely be cut to ribbons, though, after his one advantage is neutralized and he essentially winds up playing the other guy's game.

My pal Bob Rosburg once told me about how one big-hitter beat this hustle. It happened at Paradise Valley in Scottsdale, where a guy named Al Biscott talked Earl Mitchell into this bet. Biscott was winning every hole, until Earl got wise and hit his next tee shot in the opposite direction of the green. That turned the hole into about 700 yards, and after that Biscott had no chance to keep up with Mitchell.

Pretty tricky, huh? Well you know golfers . . .

Hangtime

Some hustlers carry a stopwatch to the golf course and propose bets for the "Longest Time in the Air." After a few somewhat equal bets, the mark is convinced that no ball can be kept airborne for more than five or six seconds.

Then the hustler says, "I didn't do it myself, but I know of someone who hit a regulation golf ball off flat ground (not into the Grand Canyon or anything) and it stayed in the air over 10 seconds—and I can prove it."

Whatever you do, *Don't call this bet.* You're being hustled.

When astronaut Alan Shepard hit his six-iron on the moon, the ball traveled roughly 240 yards. What isn't widely known is how long the ball stayed in the air. In that atmosphere, gravity's pull was roughly six times less than on earth, and Alan told me the ball was airborne for about 20 seconds.

One small step for mankind will lead to one wager lost.

Another pal of mine, Ed Bruce, the country-and-western singer, tells a story of another kind of hustle. Con Hunley, who like Ed is a c&w picker, set up a game in Knoxville, Tennessee, with a friend named Earl. Con asked Earl if he could bring his father along, and Earl said that would be fine. Con said, "Earl, since Daddy doesn't know anything about golf, he might say something stupid. But whatever he does, please don't embarrass him." Being a gentleman, Earl agreed to bite his tongue.

On the way to the course for the match, Con told his dad that he would enjoy watching and learning about golf. He also told his dad to say some encouraging words to Earl every time he was starting to swing. Not knowing any better, Con's dad agreed.

On the first tee, Con hit a good drive down the middle. Earl prepared to hit, and in the middle of his backswing, Con's dad blurted out, "Hit it hard, Earl." Ruffled, Earl sliced the ball into the rough. On the greens, in the middle of Earl's backstroke, Con's dad would call out, "You can make this one, Earl."

Earl never said a word to Con's dad, but on the 8th tee, Earl collared Con. "You dad is the sweetest old man in the world, Con, and I wouldn't hurt his feelings for anything," Earl said. "But if I pay you $100 right now, will you get him to go home after the front nine?"

Ten Feet of String

Dub Tyler who lives at Hideaway Lake in East Texas used to take on real good golfers under the conditions he could use "ten feet of string."

As Dub explained it to his opponent, if he had a 20-foot putt and left it 3 feet short, he would cut off 3 feet of his string and count the putt as made. In theory, Dub would run out of string somewhere during the round.

In practice, though, that seldom happened. A lot of good players got hustled by Dub in this game. In the first place, Dub was a good player himself. Second, his misses were more likely to be three inches than three feet. He made a lot of putts to start with and didn't use much string on the others.

While his opponents thought the string might amount to three or four shots a round, it usually worked out to nine or 10. Dub shot in the mid-70s to start with, and using Ten Feet of String, he was nearly always in the mid-60s. That was hard for anyone to beat.

I guess you could say Dub gave them enough rope—or in this case, string—to hang themselves.

By the way, I've also heard of club tournaments where each entrant is given a certain length of string to help with his round, usable wherever it's deemed appropriate. Other than on short putts, another good use of the string is to inch away from bad lies or from under the lip of a trap.

Me Me Me

This game was invented by my pal Jerry Biesel. In essence, by saying "Me, Me, Me," Biesel was proposing a low ball match against three separate players in which he would play three separate balls.

What Jerry's opponents failed to take into consideration was that Biesel could "go to school" on every shot.

Since his tee shots would generally fall in the same area, he could be certain of his club selection on his second and third shots. His opponents might over-club or under-club but Jerry seldom did.

On the greens, giving Jerry three balls to putt was like giving Willie Sutton the combination to the bank safe. He'd get the feel of the greens and the pace and wear people out.

When Biesel said, "Me, Me, Me," other players should have answered in unison, "No, No, No."

Drinking Games

Drink Up Your Handicap

This drinking game favors the player who can hold his liquor.

The action begins at the 19th hole, rather than the first tee. A player can add a stroke to his handicap for each beer—or highball—he consumes before the round begins.

Say you're a 9-handicapper. If you so choose, you can down six beers before the round and play to a 15 that day.

The risk you run, of course, is that the six beers by themselves will turn you into a 20-handicapper—or worse.

I've observed through the years that many casual golfers play better after they've had a pop or two. The booze relieves tension and helps them relax during a round.

These people will benefit the most from Drink Up Your Handicap, since it has a positive effect both on their swing and their handicap.

I especially like the concept behind this game, since it combines two of my favorite sports.

Sniff & Snort

Sniff & Snort is a sensational game for golfers who like a taste of whiskey or for whiskey drinkers who like a taste of golf.

Sniff & Snort was a traditional game played by Gary Smith and his buddies at the Smilk Beach course in Mt. Vernon, Washington.

At the first tee, they'd break the seal on a bottle of spirits and everyone in the group took a snort. (Mixers in the golf cart were optional.)

Thereafter, only the winner of the hole got to take a snort. The other player or players could only sniff the bottle.

After a player has won several consecutive holes and had several snorts, his motor skills tend to be affected and the other player or players see their fortunes improve. It was a self-policing kind of handicap.

I must say this absolutely sounds like my kind of game. I'll take either Phil Harris or Dean Martin as my partner and we'll play the field.

Blindman

This is a 19th hole game that tests a golfer's familiarity with the course. A player is blindfolded and taken to a tee, where he is told he must find the cup on that hole within 30 minutes. The bet is whether he will or won't make it in the alloted time.

The player is informed which tee he is standing on and then spun around several times to disorient him. Then he is turned loose, and using his sense of distance and direction and accompanied by aides who steer him out of the way of trees and other hazards, his job is to proceed to the hole as fast as possible and find the cup. (The flagstick is removed to add to the degree of difficulty.)

If the golfer has played the hole that day, having the flagstick removed doesn't add too much difficulty. But if he hasn't been on the course, finding the green can be the easy part; finding the cup can take forever when you have no inkling where it might be.

The people participating in the bet typically tag along as the gallery. In some games, they are permitted to hassle or misdirect the blindfoldee. Most behave in a gentlemanly fashion, however, since they realize the day is coming when they'll have the blinders on.

Personally, I'd rather play golf or gin rummy than walk around in the dark. I've heard that one group had the blindman so turned around that before they could stop him he walked into a lake. I suspect this game was dreamed up by the food and beverage manager, because you know spectators don't follow the action empty-handed.

Pound Notes

On cold days in Scotland, the Scottish play golf. On really cold days, they still play golf.

But on chill-your-bones, freeze-your-ass kind of days the Scottish stay in the 19th hole and play a game called Pound Notes.

They're not crazy, you know.

Pound Notes are similar to U.S. dollar bills, except they have only six ID numbers on them. The game is played between two players comparing numbers in sequence. Low numbers win, just as in golf.

If one player has a note marked 426931 and the second player's note is 114287, the first player loses the first four holes and wins the last two holes.

Since each Pound Note has six numbers, or holes, three notes constitute an 18-hole match.

Then the players have a pint of lager, pull out another Pound Note and "have another go at it, me lads."

Coach

This popular 19th hole game tests the prowess of a good golfer to convey his trade secrets to a high-handicapper.

In the game of Coach, two scratch players (or low-handicappers) wager that they will do the best job of coaching a high-handicapper player.

The Coaches have one week to work with their proteges. Then an 18-hole match ensues the following week.

The bet is won by the Coach whose player shoots the best score adjusted for handicap. The Coach cannot play any of the shots, of course, but can help in club selection, reading greens, and overall strategy.

As in any "duel," a good amount of side action can be expected to accompany a game of Coach.

Pool Bets

Most people have "bought a square" to take part in an office or bar pool bet, usually for a football game. The bet adds some viewer interest while the game is being played.

It probably won't surprise you much to learn that you can bet on golfers in golf tournaments just as easily.

One of the best pool bets is for a four-day PGA Tour or Senior PGA Tour event. It employs a deck of cards and individual bets on eleven players and the rest of the field.

Have twelve people put $20 each in a pot. Then take out all the cards of one suit (spades, for example) and set aside the king. Using the ace through queen, have the people draw to see who gets to draft first (ace) second (the deuce) all the way to twelfth (queen). The final player is left with the field bet (unless someone chose the field earlier). Whoever has the winner gets the entire pot.

Another fun pool bet can be played at the 19th hole while watching the TV coverage of a tournament like The Masters.

Using the deck of cards for the "draft," everyone picks a player. Then a point system is used to settle bets.

If your golfer makes eagle, everyone in the game owes you $20. If he makes birdie, they all owe you $5. Pars are worth nothing either way. But you owe everyone else $5 for bogies, $10 for double bogies and $20 for triples or worse.

TV coverage of major events like The Masters is so thorough that it's fairly easy to keep up with the hole-by-hole scores of the final dozen players.

Practice Games

Scrambler's Delight

This is a terrific practice game for low-handicappers and scratch players. Jack Fleck, who stunned the golf world by beating Ben Hogan in a playoff for the 1955 U.S. Open, told me about this one.

Fleck said Scrambler's Delight became a popular game in the late '60s at Mission Viejo in California, and it's still played regularly in several parts of the country.

As you might surmise, the object of Scrambler's Delight is to win holes by getting up and down. If a player hits a green in regulation he automatically *loses* the hole. The trick is to hit the fringe, or in a bunker, and then outscramble your opponent.

There are some guys, like Tom Watson or Seve Ballesteros, you'd never want to play at this game. Gary Player is another one. This is a good game to play because it reveals how solid your short game really is. It's also one of the few games where you can learn something about golf course management, where to hit the ball to set up the chip or pitch.

Incidentally, the best course manager I ever saw was Doug Ford, the 1957 Masters champion. Ford could play a course one time and then go into the 19th hole and tell guys who'd been members for years things they didn't know about their own course.

When someone mentions Scrambler's Delight, I think about the time a sportswriter in Los Angeles bet Sam Snead a thousand dollars that the Slammer couldn't play 18 holes with 18 or less putts. Sam took the bet and basically played his own Scrambler's Delight. He'd miss the green then use a pitch and a putt to get up-and-down.

On the front nine, Sam had eight one-putt greens and chipped in on one hole. The reporter promptly offered him $500 to settle and was greatly relieved when Sam accepted.

Sam was satisfied, too, because he knew better than anyone how tough it would have been to repeat that performance for 9 more holes. Try it yourself sometime and see what happens.

Backyard Golf

This is a simple, but effective practice game, suggested by Ben Smith, the Senior PGA Tour player.

In Backyard Golf, golfers move back as far as possible behind the tees, even standing in the woods, to lengthen the course.

It's not a good practice game for scoring, obviously, but Backyard Golf forces a player to hit all the shots in the bag. You'll find yourself getting plenty of practice with fairway woods and long irons, areas in which most games need strengthening. It's not hard to stretch a course to more than 8,000 yards.

Best of Two Shots

As opposed to Worst of Two (see Hustlers' Games), Best of Two is fun. It's a good game for individuals or twosomes to play, since it won't hold up play.

You hit two balls on every shot and play the best of the two. It's a simple game and an enjoyable one, too, because players are bound to shoot a good score.

The practice value comes into play because players are allowed to hit repeat shots and correct errors they might have made on the first swing.

I can think of a couple of British Opens in particular where I would have liked to play this game for real.

Thru The Trap

This is a practice game Chuck Reibling and his teammates at Ohio State University used to play to improve their sand skills.

On the tee at every hole, the players would pick out a bunker that they would play through en route to the hole.

The game didn't do much for their scores, obviously, but it did help toughen them up.

Among other things, Thru The Trap taught the OSU crowd when to be defensive on their approach shots. They learned from experience which bunkers you *never* want to visit. Every course has a few . . .

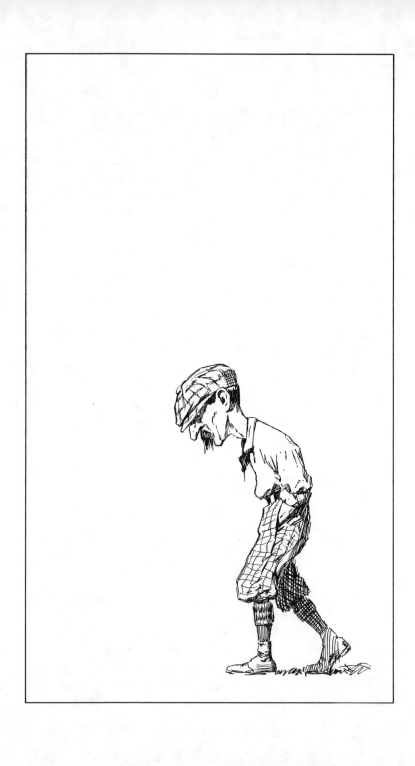

You Bet Your (Golfing) Life

I've been playing golf professionally since 1956, the year I won the Canadian Open as an amateur just shy of my 23rd birthday. I turned pro on Pearl Harbor Day in 1956 and made my debut on the PGA Tour in June 1957 after spending the winter and spring months of that year playing the Caribbean circuit. By the time I left the tour in the mid-1970s, I had won 20 PGA tournaments, the last of which was the 1972 Kemper Open, made thousands of friends and earned nearly a million dollars in prize money. And, as the popular line goes, I spent nearly ten million dollars making one million.

With the advent of the PGA Senior Tour in the 1980s, and with my having blown out 50 candles on the birthday cake my wife, Scotty, baked for me on July 24, 1983, I have returned to playing competitive golf full-time. Shoot, I was ready for this a long time ago—my body was 50 at least fifteen years earlier.

The PGA Senior Tour has reunited me with my boys of summer—Sam Snead, Arnold Palmer, Don January, Miller Barber, Gary Player, and Chi-Chi Rodriguez and believe me, we're having the times of our lives. Galleries flock to see us play, corporate sponsors identify with us, the TV cameras are pointed our way again and the prize money we're competing for is as much as the regular PGA Tour offered when I stopped playing full-time in the early 1970s.

From one event—The Legends of Golf—in 1978, the Senior PGA Tour in less than a decade has become the hottest game in town. And with great players joining the ranks each year, the Tour promises to get bigger and bigger. We PGA Seniors have discovered that life begins again at 50. Either that or we've all died and gone to heaven.

All of which is to say I've seen just about everything there is to see in golf. My introduction to the sport goes back to when I was 7 years old and discovered that toting golf clubs around a golf course beat the heck out of picking cotton. The moment I found out about golf caddies and learned they made more money for less work I was out of the cotton fields quicker than you could say Boll Weevil.

In my ensuing 46 years in golf, I've seen wagers of all kinds: smart ones, dumb ones, big ones, little ones, and everything else in between. One thing I've discovered is that whether the stakes are as small as a brew at the 19th hole or as large as $20,000 a hole, virtually everyone playing golf on this planet is playing for more than the exercise.

Personally, I've played golf games for five cents a hole, which was the standard bet between the caddies at the nine-hole course in my hometown of Cedartown, Georgia. I've also played golf games for five figures a hole. I've played in golf games risking my own money and in games where I was the "designated hitter" hired by someone else. I've witnessed golf games involving some of the most prominent (and recognizable) names in America in which the wagers were more than the gross national product of some Third World nations.

But of all the golf bets I've seen or heard about, the one that's most unforgettable is one that I won as a kid at my hometown course. A bunch of us caddies would have putting games for nickels and dimes and I'd usually wind up busted. I'd walk four miles up the road to our house flat broke and kicking myself for getting beat. Losing those nickel bets gave me the determination to get better, and I started practicing and practicing. Heat, cold, rain, wind—it didn't matter to me what the weather was doing, I'd be at the golf course practicing my putting and chipping. Some days the weather would be so bad the course wouldn't open for play, but there Doug Sanders would be, all by his lonesome, working on his game.

One day, when I was 11 or 12, the pro had a tournament for the caddies. And after the tournament, four of us kids each put up $5 winner take all in a putting game. Five bucks was a pretty good bankroll for a kid to be walking around with in those days. Anyway, we had a contest on the putting green, whoever sank the most putts took the pot. On that day all my practice paid off for me and I won all the money. I walked four miles home from the golf course that day with

twenty scoots in my pocket and I knew I had to be the happiest dude on the face of this earth. I doubt if my feet even needed to touch the dirt road; I was so excited I could have floated home.

The reason that one bet meant so much to me was that I had worked hard to win that game. It was no fluke. I also realized how much I liked to win. That four-mile walk from the golf course took forever after I'd lost, but when I won there was a jingle in my pocket and a bounce in my step. Taking that $15 from the other caddies taught me what it's like to win. There's not a better feeling in the world. (Well, maybe it's tied for first.)

I recall a time shortly after that when I was about 12 or 13 and for the first time my opponent was an adult, a local merchant named E.J. Dugan. We were tied playing the last hole and I was on the green in two with a putt for birdie while he was in the bunker by the green, also in two. It looked like the 25-cent Nassau we were playing for was mine. Well, Mr. Dugan promptly knocked his sand shot smack dab into the cup. Now I had to make a 20-footer just to halve the match.

As I stood over the putt I began to shake. There was a dryness in my mouth and I could barely swallow. Then it dawned on me what was happening—I was choking. I took the putter back and hit that ball as hard as I could and it barely made it halfway to the hole. I told myself trudging home that night that it was the last time I was going to choke.

I adopted a positive attitude immediately after that match. I told myself that from then on even when I miss putts—and I've missed hundreds of them, including that memorable one at the British Open— it won't be because I choked. I intend to burn the center of the cup every time I take the putter back.

Since that day in Cedartown, I've looked Old Man Choke right in the eye and laughed in his face. I've kept a positive approach about everything I do, whether playing golf in a Seniors Tour event, making a business deal or trying to raise funds for charity, which I do with the Doug Sanders Celebrity Classic in Houston each spring. People who think like winners and act like winners have a chance to be winners. It's true in life and it's damn sure true in golf.

Being positive about yourself and your game is the best advice I can offer any player. (Either that, or shorten your backswing!) The psychology is simple: If you believe you can execute a shot or make a putt, you at least have a chance of doing so; but if you harbor any doubts about executing the shot, you'll miss it.

Arnold Palmer's father used to tell him that a major portion of the game of golf is played from the shoulders up, meaning attitude or mental approach. Or as Yogi Berra said about baseball, but what is applicable to all professional sports, "Half the game is 90 percent mental."

Now that you've been introduced to a variety of golf games, you should be able to select some that are best suited for you. Evaluate yourself, your opponents, evaluate the alternative games and pick one or two that favor *your* game. Only make your opponent think it's his game, too.

It's important to stay on your toes during a round. Think like a winner: If you come to a dogleg left and you've been hooking the ball well that day, press your advantage. But if a hole is a dogleg right and your opponent is a natural fader and you've been hooking are you going to press? Are you going to accept his press? I wouldn't. If your opponent is rolling the ball smoothly on the practice green and your putter feels like a crowbar in your hands, what are you going to say when he suggests a side bet on fewest putts? No or hell no.

Incidentally, a lot of people think a golfer is being a wimp if he doesn't press when he has the chance. Those people believe a player should always press when he has the opportunity, like being 2-down or whatever. Let me just say that a golfer can go broke listening to that sort of advice.

Face it, the magic doesn't always work. Some days you won't be able to execute any shot the way you intend to. The clubs will feel uncomfortable, the swing will seem out of rhythm, the putts won't fall—nothing will be going your way.

On those days, you should keep your bets to a minimum. One of my favorite sayings is "Just because you hear the music doesn't mean you have to dance." If your favorite dance is the waltz but the band is playing the foxtrot—don't cut in on the dance floor.

The single most important quality you must have if you're playing golf for money is Patience with a capital P. Don't force the action, let things come naturally. There will come a day when everything works to your advantage. You'll be feeling sharp and you'll be concentrating well.

Your opponents will seem preoccupied with business or in a hurry. Maybe they're hung over from too much partying the night before. When things are going your way, take advantage of them. It's like when you have hot dice in your hand in Las Vegas—you go with the flow. It's like knowing when it's time to double or triple your bets at the blackjack table.

When the advantages point to you, let it all hang out. When they point the other way, trim your sails and cut your losses. That's all a matter of money management.

I'm talking about natural advantages here, not skullduggery. I'm not talking about resorting to chicanery. Like asking your opponent things like, "When did you change to a hook grip?" just before you come to a series of straight holes. Or "When did you move the ball forward in your putting stance?" as you come to a difficult green.

Those sorts of comments can plant seeds of doubt in the mind of any golfer. They'll gnaw away on confidence like it's a big turkey leg. Of course, gentlemen golfers don't do those sorts of things. Hustlers might, but they're out there for one reason, and one reason only, to get your money.

If you're playing with a regular group, you have to exercise some care in how you win. You can't clobber your playing partners, or they'll go find another group. You've got to take their measure without breaking their spirit. If you find yourself way ahead, make an extra bet with an adjustment of strokes. Give the man a chance.

My advice for any golfer is always play to win. Someone once said, "Winning isn't the only thing, but it beats the hell out of whatever's next," and I absolutely agree. My point in discussing golf gambling is simply this: Always play to win, but on some days don't win any bigger than you have to.

There's something else to mention. Golfers are competitors and golf games are extremely competitive. But don't go overboard in your zest to be the best in your group.

I'd like to suggest some hard and fast rules for people who read this book to follow. These are Doug Sanders' guidelines to golf gambling.

1. Never gamble to hurt a friend.

What's more important to you, a friendship or one lousy bet? Play to win, bet to win, but don't hustle your friends. If you want to hammer someone go to an unfamiliar course and put a whipping on an absolute stranger. But don't be trying to break the spirit of your friends, unless you'll be satisfied to have a small number of them.

2. Never gamble outside your comfort zone.

Golfers tend to overestimate their abilities. They also tend to let their egos dominate their rational minds. As a result, they get corralled into making some bets or playing for higher stakes than they should

(remember the poor guy in the game of Roll 'em?). The best players are those who can manage themselves and their money. They keep a tight rein on themselves and on their check books. They are aware that there's always somebody ready to come along and play a little bit better.

In the late 1950s, Ben Smith, one of my buddies on the Senior PGA Tour, hooked up in a match with an Atlanta fireman who was the resident hot-shot at a local municipal course called Chandler Park. Ben won three $15 bets that day—a lot of money to both players. When they came into the clubhouse the fireman was so hot, so to speak, that Ben kept quiet and didn't ask for his money. He watched as the fireman pulled out a knife with a 6-inch blade and proceeded to cut up his golf pants. Then he sliced up his golf shoes and threw them

into a tree outside the clubhouse. Then the fireman hacked up his golf bag. Finally, the fireman sold his clubs to the pro, Chicken Yates, and paid Ben Smith the $45 and left without saying another word. Chicken Yates said he never saw the fireman back at the course after that. It's safe to say the fireman was a casualty of betting beyond the comfort zone.

3. Never needle, harrass or poke fun at a playing partner who's on the edge of despair.

Friendly banter is part of the golfing experience. Misery loves company, after all. But common courtesy dictates that you not kick a partner when he's down. Take your cues from your opponent. If he's able to laugh at himself and his own misfortune, then by all means add your sarcasm and caustic wit to the proceedings. But if the poor guy is being so humbled that his head is hanging down and his lips are sealed, give him a break.

And if he's really steaming, keep quiet until he cools off. Nearly anything that's said in those heated moments will be remembered far after the circumstances are forgotten. It's a good policy to say nothing until the storm subsides.

4. Never fail to settle your debts immediately after a round.

It's alarming the number of golfers who don't come prepared to cover their debts. IOU's don't cut it on the golf course. Save your chits for the card games in the 19th hole. That's why some games like Oklahoma Whip–Out require a settlement at the end of each hole. When there's hot and heavy action all around, it's a good policy to follow.

5. If you're the winner, be a gracious one.

The 19th hole is a place where the winner should willingly part with some of his gains and buy a round (three or four if I'm the loser) for his vanquished foes. It's a good time to savor the spoils of victory.

On other occasions, you need to make a discreet exit. One of those for me came in the early 1960s at the Odessa Pro-Am. Odessa in those days was a hotbed of golf gambling and you could get all kinds of action. I had accepted a few sporting propositions on the golf course and in the card room as well.

That year my amateur partner was Richard Crawford, the NCAA champion from the University of Houston. On the final day we were paired with Jackson Bradley, the pro at River Oaks C.C. in Houston and his partner, Homero Blancas, another University of Houston star.

Crawford and I were competing not only in the overall tournament, but we also had some serious side bets riding on the outcome of our match with Bradley and Blancas. And for some reason a lot of the folks in Odessa had bet against us—although I'm sure it had nothing to do with how my luck had been running at the card table.

As we came to the 18th hole, Richard and I were even on a few bets, down a half-shot on some more bets and down one shot on a few more. If we finished that way we figured to lose about $7,000. The first prize in the tournament, I should point out, was considerably less than that.

I reached the green on the par-4 in two, but my birdie putt was going to be a tough 20-foot sidehill number. Jackson hit to about the same distance away and then Homero hit one stiff to the pen. He had a two-foot putt for birdie, a virtual lock.

The tournament was being shown on closed-circuit TV in the clubhouse and when the Odessa oilmen saw Homero's shot they went wild. "We got that sonofabitch Sanders this time," they shouted. Indeed, it looked pretty grim. Even if we birdied the hole to match Homero, we still would lose $7,000. If we failed to birdie and lost the 18th hole outright, out debts would be considerably higher.

So what did Dick Crawford do? He hit a wedge off the hardpan from 100 yards out and landed the ball just short of the green. It bounced once or twice, rolled forward and promptly disappeared into the hole for an eagle two. There was a swing of about $20,000 on the hole, and you could hear the screams of the Odessa oilmen all the way to Midland.

A locker room attendant named A. Z. Sanders, whom I jokingly called

"Namesake," came out of the club and whispered to me that I should keep a lid on my victory gloating.

"Mister Doug," said Namesake. "Get your money and then get on down the road."

It seems everyone in the locker room went nuts when Crawford's shot dropped in the hole. I mean they totally trashed the place. Someone threw his golf shoe through the TV screen and things generally went downhill from there. It was a time for me to collect my winnings quietly and ease on down the road. The clubhouse damages in Odessa, I later learned, came to more than $3,000.

Anyway, if you play golf long enough, you will have many rich experiences of your own to look back on and maybe laugh at. The main thing I hope you've derived from reading *Doug Sanders' Action on the First Tee* is an increased sense of the many ways to enjoy the game of golf.

Like I said at the beginning, variety is the spice of life. Now you've got a heap of variety to add to your golf game. So go ahead and be a tiger on the first tee.

Alphabetical Index to Golf Gambling Games